Thank You for the Mountain

How to conquer your defeated money mindset to achieve financial freedom

Copyright © 2025 Alicia Fitts

All rights reserved. No part of this publication may be reproduced, distributed, or transmitted in any form or by any means, including photocopying, recording, or other electronic or mechanical methods, without the prior written permission of the publisher, except in the case of brief quotations embodied in critical reviews and certain other noncommercial uses permitted by copyright law. For permission requests, write to the publisher, addressed "Attention: Permissions Coordinator," at the address below.

Print ISBN: 978-1-63616-214-0
eBook ISBN: 978-1-63616-215-7

Published By Opportune Independent Publishing Co.
www.opportunepublishing.com

Printed in the United States of America

For permission requests, please email the publisher with the subject line as "Attention: Permissions Coordinator"
to the email address below:
Info@Opportunepublishing.com

PRE-ORDER ACKNOWLEDGMENT LIST

Terrell Fitts
Brenda Walden
Michael L. Walden
Michael & Juanita Walden
Cynthia McKinley
Lashantel Pinckney
Dr. Greg Shields
Leticia Salazar
Tanga Fitts
Claudine Carlisle-Green
Brooke Westbrook
Denise Brown
Tammy Gordon
Fergie Chanel Willis
Dora Walden
Lynn Cobb
Dennise Fitts
Christian Cunningham
Andrea Bennett
Leo & Joyce Dennison
Angienieka West
Maria Cook
Leroy & Cassandra Rogers
Nikia Johnson
Thelma Crain
Tawanaca Williams
Teresa Cobb
Nikki Brigham
Melisa Clark
Sean & Tina D'Antignac
Kim Danner
Laray Avery
Virginia Hall
Develon Davis
Victor Timothy Wynn
Mark Walden
Marcus Walden
Corey Johnson
Akiesha Taylor
Myna Shegog
Jada Haynes
GiGi Lewis
Tamekia Fallin
Dr. Bobbie Youmans
Bishop Mark Walden
Mother CJ Walden
Nanette Barnes
Keisha Quick
Lindsay Black
LaRissa Briggs
Joyce Duty
Lonnie Childs
Judge Ashanti Lilley Pounds
Tywone Thomas
Odell Cleveland
Sherri Chance
Vondesa Lee
Dwanette Pullings
Rysheeka Bush
Mary Allen

DEDICATION

First and foremost, I dedicate this book to God. His divine instruction led me to write this book to help a generation of people. I admit, I was hesitant to share my struggles, but God made it clear that my deliverance would come through helping others. By sharing my pain with vulnerability, I desire to provide hope and strategies for others to overcome their challenges because, with God, all things are possible.

ACKNOWLEDGMENTS

In life, God blesses us with destiny helpers, so I dedicate this book to the following angels who have been instrumental in its completion.

To my husband, Terrell Fitts, and amazing children, Noah, Evan, and Cassidy Fitts.

To my loving and supportive parents, Michael and Brenda Walden.

To my wonderful siblings, Michael David Walden, Marcus Walden, and Mark Walden and Juanita Walden.

To my angelic godmother, Bobbie Sue Wilson.

To all those supporting my journey as an author, especially those who preordered this book.

It truly takes a village, empowerment through collaboration! With God, nothing (and I mean nothing) is impossible if you believe in Him and His miracle-working power!

IT'S TIME TO GO FROM
VISION TO VICTORY

TURNING GOD-GIVEN DREAMS INTO REAL-WORLD SUCCESS

LEGACY BUILDERS
FINANCIAL COACHING PROGRAM

PURPOSE TO PROFIT
BUSINESS MENTORSHIP PROGRAM

BRAND NEW DAY
PERSONAL BRAND DEVELOPMENT COACHING PROGRAM

WITH MANY YEARS OF EXPERIENCE AS A BUSINESS AND MARKETING PROFESSIONAL ALICIA IS READY TO SERVE YOU FOR YOUR WEALTH & BRANDING NEEDS.

ALICIA FITTS IS A CHRISTIAN BUSINESS COACH, WEALTH & BRANDING STRATEGIST, AND CERTIFIED FINANCIAL EDUCATOR.

HER CONSULTING FIRM IS READY TO TURN YOUR DREAMS INTO REALITY AND HELP YOU BUILD A LEGACY OF SUCCESS.

READY TO START? VISIT
WWW.ALICIAFITTS.COM
TO LEARN MORE OR SCHEDULE YOUR FREE CONSULTATION TODAY!

ALICIA FITTS FOUNDER/CEO

CONTENTS

Introduction
God's Hierarchy of Needs..................................11

Chapter 1 - *Featuring Michael Walden*
Acceptance, Accountability & Action......................13

Chapter 2 - *Featuring Tamekia Fallin*
It's Never Too Late to Create a Budget....................37

Chapter 3 - *Featuring Pastor Odell Cleveland*
Money & Marriage..61

Chapter 4 - *Featuring Bishop Mark Walden*
Money & Kingdom Mindset.................................93

Chapter 5 - *Featuring Sherri Chance & Vondesa Lee*
Planning for Life's Major Events........................117

Chapter 6 - *Featuring Tywone Thomas*
Entrepreneurship & Streams of Income...................145

About the Author 171

Thank You for the Mountain

INTRODUCTION
GOD'S HIERARCHY OF NEEDS

"In the last days the mountain of the Lord's temple will be established as the highest of the mountains; it will be exalted above the hills, and all nations will stream to it. Many people will come and say, 'Come, let us go up to the mountain of the Lord, to the temple of the God of Jacob. He will teach us his ways, so that we may walk in his paths.' The law will go out from Zion, the word of the Lord from Jerusalem." - Isaiah 2:2-3

Chapter 1

Acceptance, Accountability & Action

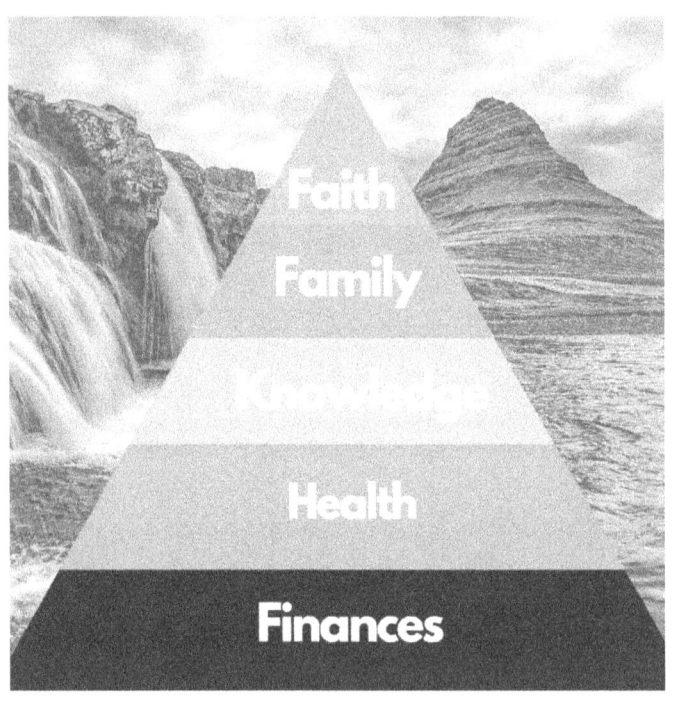

If you've picked up this book, chances are you desire to improve your relationship with your finances. I want to congratulate you on taking an important first step toward moving the needle forward in your financial life. This step can lead you to attain financial success. I know this because I have been there too. Please allow me to introduce myself. My name is Alicia Fitts, and I am an experienced certified credit union financial counselor. It wasn't until I endured the most difficult and driest financial seasons in my life that I woke up.

One day, I realized I had to take accountability for my situation. My family was suffering financially. Simply dreaming and hoping for a change would not create results, so I quickly learned that I could not rely on anyone else to find the solution. I had to take action and be the solution.

I noticed a remarkable difference in my circumstances after I enhanced my relationship with the Lord. God provided me with the map for my exodus out of financial bondage. In this book, I share the lessons and tools that helped my family push through what felt like one of the darkest seasons of our lives.

Dealing with financial struggles was particularly challenging for me. If it had just been my problem, it might have been easier to manage. But there were three young children under the age of five depending on me and my husband to provide for them. This reality activated a different level of drive and ambition in me. I could not let them down, so my actions had to reflect my commitment to their well-being.

I didn't inherit wealth from my family. However, I saw my parents work hard. They endeavored to provide the best they could for me and my three siblings. My parents set a high standard, and I wanted to follow their example. Little did I know that much of what they provided involved sacrifices. Their journey included seasons of lack. The foundation they laid was centered around faith, family, and education, yet there was one vital topic missing in this foundational formula: finances. I do not fault my parents for me not knowing much about financial literacy. I also do not blame the government or school systems for my lack of financial knowledge. Life is busy. With all of its distractions, fitting the topic of finances into our conversations can be challenging. My parents juggled raising four children, working full-time jobs, and being faithful to their church commitments.

Like many families today, a number of us often become overwhelmed with bills. We fail to prioritize equipping our children with the financial literacy they need. As parents, we might set up a trust, create a certificate of deposit, or establish a college fund. These are wonderful financial tools. However, what good are they if we do not have conversations about finances? Our children must learn to be good stewards of their money.

We need to have open discussions about spending, saving, and investing. This education is crucial. It teaches young people how to manage their resources wisely. Let us not overlook the significance of starting these conversations early.

I have reframed my parents' foundational formula

to include faith, family, education, finances, and fitness. In today's world, financial literacy is crucial. We cannot allow it to be an afterthought any longer. According to Cerulli Associates, up to $68 trillion will move between generations within the next 25 years (1). This is a staggering amount of money. The upcoming wealth transfer from the baby boomer generation will be immense, but what good is this transfer if the heirs do not possess the right tools or knowledge?

Yes, Generation X, millennials, and Generation Z can hire financial advisors. However, as stated in James 1:5 (NIV), "If any of you lacks wisdom, you should ask God, who gives generously to all without finding fault, and it will be given to you." Our first step should be to depend on God for wisdom and knowledge to handle wealth transfer effectively. I am a millennial. Whether we are heirs or not, understanding finances is essential for everyone. Financial literacy is crucial for navigating life, whether we are rich or poor.

We are on a divine assignment, and the next generation needs to learn about God's formula for success. Through my personal journey, I have seen how following this divine formula has helped my family endure tough times. Jeremiah 32:17 (NIV) states, "Ah, Sovereign Lord, you have made the heavens and the earth by your great power and outstretched arm. Nothing is too hard for you." This truth affirms our faith in God's ability to guide us.

I will focus specifically on millennials now. As of January 2022, millennials—those born between 1981 and 1996—face significant levels of debt, which primarily arises from several factors. Student loans are a major issue. Credit card debt is another challenge millennials face, and the rising cost of living adds to financial strain. Understanding how to manage these debts is crucial for financial health and success.

The Current Financial Distress Situation

Debt is an insidious reality that many millennials face today. As a mother and a member of this generation, I understand how crushing it can feel. Let's look at some of the major types of debt and financial challenges that millennials experience.

1. Student Loans
Student loans represent a crucial turning point in a person's financial landscape, particularly for millennials. We enter higher education feeling eager and ambitious, yet many of us emerge with debts that feel like chains, shackling us to a daunting financial future. The pain is real. The pressure mounts as we juggle our dreams for a better life alongside crippling student loans. According to recent statistics, the total student loan debt in the U.S. has surpassed $1.7 trillion, with millennials bearing the heaviest load (2). This staggering figure isn't just a number; it symbolizes the struggle and anxiety that infiltrates everyday life.

Understanding student loans means confronting the harsh truth behind them. For many of us, this debt results from pursuing degrees in hopes of securing stable jobs. Yet, we often find ourselves in entry-level positions that barely cover our living expenses, not making a dent in our loan payments. When faced with this situation, the emotional weight is almost unbearable. I recall the days when I struggled to make minimum loan payments while grocery shopping with my children, wishing every item could simply go on hold until payday. The guilt of not providing a secure financial environment for my little ones gnawed at me. Each overdue notice felt like another brick added to a wall of despair.

We have a tendency to defer responsibility, but we must face it. Acceptance is our first step. We cannot ignore our financial situation any longer. It is time to take accountability for our loans and learn from our choices. Why did we borrow so much money? Each of us has a unique story—whether it was the promise of a bright future or simply a lack of financial knowledge. Remember, collective pain births powerful lessons.

The reality is that our education is an investment. Unlike traditional investments, student loans often go hand-in-hand with interest rates averaging about 6.5% to 9% for federal loans (3). This burden grows heavier over time. Consider this: If you have $30,000 in student loans at this interest rate, you could be looking at nearly $400 per month in payments. This is money that could be diverted toward essential needs like childcare or housing.

2. Credit Card Debt
Credit card debt is often an invisible weight that many millennials carry. As we juggle the demands of work, family, and finances, it can easily spiral out of control. As of 2023, millennials hold an average credit card balance exceeding $5,500 according to a report by Credit Karma

(4). This is not just a number; it reflects real-life struggles and the weight of everyday financial stress.

Many of us dive into credit card use with hopeful intentions. We enjoy the ease of plastic; a simple swipe opens avenues to convenience. But this convenience can quickly shift into chaos. High interest rates, averaging about 20%, create a cycle of debt that feels endless. Each purchase, though small, contributes to an accumulating weight that we often underestimate until the bills arrive. I remember the days when making minimum payments felt like running on a hamster wheel. I paid and paid but never seemed to make any real progress. Each month, the cycle continued. The feeling of hopelessness tightened around my chest like a vice.

Consider the anxiety you may feel when opening your credit card statement. The total comes as a shock. You may feel like you have no way out. Life becomes a series of tough decisions. Do you buy groceries this week or make that credit card payment? The guilt can be suffocating, and the desire to provide for your children may clash with feelings of inadequacy. I wondered, How can I teach about financial responsibility when I can barely handle my own debts? This internal turmoil often led to a deeper emotional crisis, leading me to worry not just about money but about my role as a provider and caregiver.

The total credit card debt in the U.S. surpasses $1 trillion, with millions of us facing the burden (5). Each story contributes to this staggering figure; we must remember there is no shame in our struggles. Instead, it is a shared experience.

3. Housing Debt
The dream of homeownership has become a distant reality for many. According to recent statistics, the total amount of outstanding mortgage debt in the U.S. has crossed $12 trillion (6). With rising interest rates and skyrocketing home prices, many people feel as though the odds are stacked against them. The housing market has changed dramatically since the 2008 financial crisis. There are stricter lending standards, and increased costs have forced many millennials to delay home purchases. It's a daunting reality that can lead to feelings of inadequacy and stress.

This struggle is often coupled with the burden of renting for longer periods. For many, renting offers little stability and eats away at savings. Every month feels like a weighty reminder of missed opportunities. The rent comes due, and it's often a painful amount. This recurring payment can feel like being on a hamster wheel—endless and exhausting. How do we choose between managing rent and saving for a down payment on a home? Often the answer feels like a cruel balancing act.

Every time the rent is paid, it's just a transaction. We are not building equity. We are simply helping someone else build their wealth while we remain trapped in a cycle of financial instability. Many of us experience anxiety each month as the due date approaches. It prompts questions about the future. You may think, Will I ever own a home? Am I failing my family? These questions are valid, yet they can burden our mental health and cloud our decision-making.

4. *Auto Loans*
Auto loans have become a common fixture in the lives of many. Millennials, more than others, are taking out loans to finance vehicles. According to Experian, the average auto loan balance for millennials as of 2023 is approximately $23,000, a significant increase that highlights how we're increasingly leaning on borrowed money for everyday necessities (7). The allure of a shiny new car can be tempting, but the reality of these loans often leaves us feeling trapped. They can lead to financial distress that seems relentless, especially as monthly payments chip away at our income.

The challenge doesn't end with the auto loan itself. Anxiety creeps in each time the payment is due. You might think to yourself, Am I making the right choice? How did it come to this? Each unpaid bill can feel like a weight on your shoulders. The loan's interest can add up, seemingly multiplying overnight. Coupled with increased living costs, the financial burden can seem overwhelming. This is not just about having a car. It's about how that vehicle can represent a larger financial struggle. We often feel like we buy convenience, not understanding the bigger picture.

Yet, in this distress, there lies an opportunity for growth. We need to reframe our mindset around auto loans. Each missed payment or financial error can become a catalyst for accountability.

5. COVID-19

The COVID-19 pandemic hit like a thunderclap. For a majority of millenials, it struck right at a time when many were already grappling with financial insecurity. One of the staggering effects of the pandemic was waves of layoffs. People felt the ground shift beneath their feet. As roughly two million millennials lost their jobs at the peak of the pandemic, many faced a grim daily reality: figuring out how to pay their rent and auto loans. Economic uncertainty casts a long shadow, making financial management feel like an impossible task.

In this crisis, the pain was visceral. It was not just about survival. It became a struggle to hold onto dreams and aspirations. Reports indicated that 3 in 10 millennials experienced increased stress about finances due to the pandemic (8). People were furloughed and forced into survival mode. This distress was not merely a number; it became a deeply felt reality.

I remember those times of financial uncertainty vividly. Each news alert about rising unemployment felt like a personal blow. Yet, amid the chaos, there existed a transformative opportunity that prompted a reevaluation of financial perspectives. Suddenly, millennials were faced with stark choices, confronting our habits and behaviors surrounding money. This was a chance to strip down our financial lives to the essentials. We were forced to think about what really mattered and rethink our priorities. Those moments of distress were cries for change, a call to transform our defeated money mindsets.

6. Financial Stress and Mental Health
The reality of financial stress among millennials is stark. As pressures mount, many find themselves battling anxiety and feeling overwhelmed. High levels of debt have profound implications on mental health. It's not just about numbers on a page. It's about lives transformed by those numbers. According to a survey by Laurel Road, nearly 72% of millennials report feeling stressed about their finances (9). This statistic isn't just a number; it's a representation of real people facing real pain. When we perceive our financial landscape as chaotic, our minds echo this chaos.

Let's delve deeper into the specifics of this distress. Imagine waking up every day with an avalanche of bills waiting to be addressed. You wonder, How will I make it this month? The weight of these thoughts can feel unbearable. A recent study published in the Journal of Family and Economic Issues indicates that high levels of financial anxiety can lead to serious health consequences, including depression and burnout. When bills pile up and decisions become paralyzing, a vicious cycle of stress can commence, inhibiting our ability to think clearly and act decisively (10).

This financial turmoil creates a significant risk for millennials. These are not isolated issues. They intertwine with our core identities. When we see ourselves as failures due to our financial standing, it disrupts sense of our self-worth. The pain becomes personal, not just financial. This reality resonates deeply.

After reviewing the information above, we must consider how to overcome the debt burden and access wealth transfer. Our generation faces a significant mountain of debt. How can we climb this mountain and find the path to financial freedom?

I have personally experienced financial struggles linked to these issues. From student loans to rising living costs, I understand the burden of debt. But I also have a clear solution. There is a process that can help millennials overcome their financial challenges. This process can help you break free from the paycheck-to-paycheck cycle and create multiple streams of income that can come from your gifts or passions.

Before you engage with this process, you must be willing to take action. You need to hold yourself accountable for your current circumstances. It is easy to feel trapped, especially when living in lack for an extended time. This feeling can cloud your vision for a better financial future. I have been there before. I know what it feels like to give everything at work yet feel overworked and undervalued. I understand how a paycheck can vanish. Bills are paid first, and there is hardly enough left for groceries. You count the days until your next payday.

I understand the frustration of wanting to save money. Yet, every time you try, an unexpected car repair hits your budget. It feels like every time you attempt to rebuild a savings or emergency fund, life throws another obstacle in your way. I also know the struggle of trying to afford daycare tuition each month. These expenses can set you back when you're already trying to keep your head above water.

Rent increases can be infuriating. I have felt the sting

of a landlord raising my rent by $100 a month, which happened simply because they could. I have also dealt with a landlord who found reasons to hold back my security deposit. It felt unfair, especially after I had been a good tenant. But God made a way for me to purchase my own home, which was a moment of joy and relief.

If you face financial challenges, remember that you are not alone. I have journeyed through many of these difficulties by utilizing the exact process described in this book. First, take a moment to reflect on your financial struggles. Write them down if it helps. Next, evaluate where you stand now. Do you see any progress? Even small steps matter. If you catch a glimpse of improvement, say out loud to God, "Thank you for the mountain!" This is a powerful expression of gratitude.

Dwelling on past mistakes will not help you move forward. Acknowledge where you are right now. You need to take responsibility for the financial choices you made that led you here. It is time to roll up your sleeves and take action. Significant and sustainable improvements in your finances are within reach.

Acceptance & Accountability

Acceptance may sound simple, but facing financial trouble is anything but easy. It is hard to admit that you need help. You may think, I need to seek out the resources and solutions for a better financial state.

Along my journey, I had all the financial knowledge imaginable. However, when the weight of overwhelming debt pressed down on me, acceptance was a challenge. Ignoring the situation only made things worse. The bills arrived like clockwork. They didn't care about my feelings. Eventually, I had to confront the reality of my situation. I could no longer run from it.

Accountability is crucial. Blaming others will not lead to financial freedom. During my awakening, I tried to point fingers. I wondered how "little Ms. Perfect" found herself in such a mess. I had a stellar credit score at age twenty-one and felt proud of my financial expertise. Yet, life can throw curve balls. I got married, switched to a job with less pay, and became pregnant almost immediately.

After countless life changes, I realized my financial issues needed direct attention. It took me five long years to learn that my burdens would not disappear until I faced them head-on. During my awakening, I took a hard look at my decisions. I understood I had switched jobs and gotten married, which impacted my finances. But I also saw that I needed a weapon in this fight—an accountability roadmap.

Creating an accountability roadmap involves a few vital steps. First, write down your financial struggles. Get specific. Do not just list the word "debt." Write how much you owe and to whom. Next, evaluate your income. List all your sources of income. Are there gaps? Identifying these gaps is crucial for understanding where to allocate your focus. Then, commemorate your small victories. If you manage to save even a dollar, celebrate. Thank God for small wins because this gratitude fuels motivation.

Establish your goals. Where do you want to be financially in six months? One year? It is imperative to set realistic objectives. Break down these goals into actionable steps. For instance, if you've identified areas where you can cut back on spending, start small. You could plan meals for the week instead of eating out. Small savings can accumulate quickly.

Accountability partners can make a massive difference. Share your goals with trusted friends or family members. They can help keep you on track. Knowing what to do is one thing. Taking those steps is another. Begin by implementing one change at a time. Maybe it's cutting out that daily coffee shop visit or opting for a home-cooked meal. These actions will create a ripple effect. As you gain momentum, your confidence will build. You will find that conquering financial issues is not just a dream but a reality waiting for you. It's about taking deliberate steps to steer your financial ship in the right direction.

Taking Action

What does taking action mean when you are overwhelmed by financial debt? It means you cannot ignore the situation any longer. You need to confront it directly. Stop blaming others. Your finances are your responsibility. I started by researching options for debt consolidation. However, I found they did not meet my needs, so I explored different paths.

Begin by gathering all your bills and credit card statements to help you see the full picture of your debt. Identify the creditors you owe. Create a clear list of amounts owed and the due dates. Next, reach out to these creditors. Do not text them. Instead, pick up the phone and have a conversation. This may seem daunting, and you might feel fear or embarrassment. But you are not alone in this struggle. According to a 2017 CareerBuilder survey, approximately 78% of American workers lived paycheck to paycheck. That includes individuals with seemingly good salaries. Understand that many are in similar situations.

When you call your creditors, be honest about your circumstances. Explain clearly what is happening. For instance, tell them if you lost your job or were faced with high unexpected expenses. Many creditors want to work with you because they want their money. I had a creditor suggest a reasonable payment plan. They even lowered my interest rate. This can happen for you too. But if you choose to do nothing, nothing will change. Take the initiative.

Credit card companies also offer balance transfers to help manage payments. This means you can move debt from a high-interest card to a low-interest one. Remember, you may need to pay a fee upfront. Also, be ready with a solid plan to tackle your debt. Do not transfer the balance without knowing how you will pay it off.

After exploring the depths of your financial situation and gaining a sense of accountability, it's time to pivot toward actionable debt strategies. Let's delve into methods that can genuinely aid your journey toward financial freedom.

1. The Snowball Method

The snowball method is all about momentum. Start by listing your debts from smallest to largest. Focus your energy on paying off the smallest debt first while making minimum payments on the others. Celebrate each win when you clear a debt. This creates a surge of motivation. You're not just reducing numbers. You are lifting that heavy weight off your shoulders one piece at a time.

For example, if you have a $500 credit card debt, pay that off first. Once it's gone, roll that payment into the next smallest debt. This strategy is incredibly empowering and reinforces your belief in your ability to overcome challenges.

2. The Avalanche Method

If you're a numbers person and want to save the most on interest, the avalanche method might resonate with you. In this approach, list your debts from the ones with the highest interest rate to the lowest. Channel your extra cash toward the debt with the highest interest. For instance, if you have a credit card charging 20% interest and another at 15%, start with the card that has a 20% interest rate. Once it's cleared, move on to the next. This strategy may take longer to see results, but the financial gains over time can be significant.

3. Debt Consolidation

Debt consolidation can be a game-changer if done correctly. This means taking multiple debts and merging them into one loan (ideally at a lower interest rate). It simplifies payments as you'll only deal with one creditor. It's crucial to ensure that the new interest rate is significantly lower; otherwise, you might end up back where you started. For example, if you consolidate multiple payments of $100 monthly into a single payment of $150, make sure the new payment fits comfortably within your budget.

Understand that this journey to financial freedom takes time. Often, it may feel like you're climbing a mountain with no summit in sight. However, each strategy you implement is a step toward the top. As you tackle your debts one strategy at a time, remember to reflect on your progress. Each small change, every strategy, works toward financial recovery and newfound confidence. Embrace the path you're on because every step, every call made to a creditor, is leading you toward a place of liberation and strength. Keep your eyes on the prize because the mountain will feel less daunting.

EXPERT HIGHLIGHT
Michael Walden

Augusta, GA
Author | Speaker | Leader
Sales & Marketing Coach | Personality
Website: www.mikelwalden.com
Podcast: Brother 2 Brother
Facebook: Michael Walden

Meet Michael Walden

Michael Walden is a seasoned Sales Representative with the Georgia Lottery Corporation, proudly serving the Augusta, Georgia region for over 27 years. In his role, he excels at managing retailer relationships, promoting lottery products, and ensuring compliance with corporate standards. His outstanding performance has earned him the prestigious MVP Award for the Georgia Lottery Augusta District twice, most recently in 2017, recognizing his excellence in sales and marketing.

In addition to his career in sales, Michael is a certified professional notary and a natural connector. Throughout his 40-year career in the CSRA, he has built strong professional relationships, using his extensive network to assist others with job opportunities and career advancement.

Michael has been married to his wife, Brenda Walden, for 36 years. Together, they have four children—three sons and one daughter—and are proud grandparents to three grandchildren, with anticipation for more to come. He has also faithfully served as an ordained Minister of Music for over 36 years, blending his love for faith and music into his life's work.

Michael credits his family as his greatest inspiration, motivating him to take action, remain accountable, and trust God for greater opportunities. His life's journey is evidence of the power of perseverance, faith, and the importance of building strong foundations—both personally and professionally.

Overcoming Defeat

Question: As a husband, father, and business professional, it's easy to feel stuck when faced with the weight of past financial mistakes. What advice would you give to someone who is struggling to accept responsibility and take the necessary steps to move forward?

Let's be honest—being stuck is a mental state, not an actual state of life. The first step toward overcoming defeat is recognizing that the way you see your situation often keeps you trapped. Once you accept this truth, you can begin shifting your mindset and expanding your perspective.

Many people experience feelings of defeat when dealing with financial hardships. However, there is a powerful strategy for turning things around: Acceptance, Accountability, and Action. Here's how:

1. Ask God for Help
James 1:5 tells us, "If any of you lacks wisdom, you should ask God, who gives generously to all without finding fault, and it will be given to you." God often works through people—financial counselors, trusted friends, mentors—so don't be afraid to seek guidance.

2. Acknowledge Your Problems—Don't Ignore Them
Ignoring financial hardships only delays your breakthrough. Most financial problems stem from spending more than you earn. Recognize that change is needed: cut unnecessary expenses and seek additional sources of income if necessary.

I remember having to make a hard decision as a father of four small children. I knew it was time for a career shift when I realized my hard work was not being valued. My wife, who was a stay-at-home mom, returned to work as a substitute teacher to help make ends meet. Those were tough times—we faced everything from plumbing issues to having more month than money.

But I trusted God. I cut grass with a friend to provide for my family. Eventually, God opened a door that led to a 27-year career with the Georgia Lottery Corporation—one that allowed us to move from a struggling neighborhood to building a home in a dream community. What seemed impossible at the time became a testimony of what happens when you combine accountability with action.

3. Activate Your Faith

I married the love of my life, Brenda Joyce Walden, on August 12, 1989. Together, we raised four wonderful children—our "Fantastic Four." Each one became a first-generation college graduate, taking different paths but all staying the course to finish their journeys.

We taught our children to put God first, to walk in integrity, and to work hard. They didn't use our lack of college degrees as an excuse to give up. They took responsibility for their futures—and they succeeded.

Hebrews 11:1 says, "Now faith is the substance of things hoped for, the evidence of things not seen."

Faith in action can change your entire life. Early in my career, while working as a traffic engineer for the

City of Augusta, I used to patrol a beautiful, exclusive neighborhood filled with dream homes. I told my riding partner, "One day, I'm going to live here." He laughed and said I couldn't even afford a garage on our salary.

But I kept believing. I would drive through that neighborhood every Sunday after church, speaking life over my dream. Only my youngest son, Mark, would walk the lots with me at six years old, believing alongside me.

Eventually, God provided. I took on extra jobs, and He opened doors for better employment opportunities. After much perseverance—and a little negotiation from my wife—we purchased land in that very neighborhood and built our dream home.

We went from squeezing a family of six into one Toyota Corolla and living paycheck to paycheck, to raising college graduates, welcoming grandchildren, and living comfortably in a home we once thought was out of reach.

If God could do it for me and my family, He can surely do it for you.

Stay faithful, take action, and refuse to stay stuck. Your mountain can be moved!

CHAPTER 2

It's Never Too Late to Create a Budget

Now more than ever, it is critical to establish a budget, regardless of your status: single, married, or married with children. A proper budget will allow you to assess your monthly fixed and variable expenses. A fixed expense remains constant from month to month, such as rent or mortgage payments, while variable expenses fluctuate, like utility bills and the cost of groceries. Once you have established a budget, it is essential to reevaluate it each month. Don't expect your budget to remain the same every month.

A budget will help you avoid additional fees from banks or creditors, which can cause your finances to spiral downward. Trust me, when you're living paycheck to paycheck, overdraft fees can be a nightmare. You do not want to give those fees any credit, which makes it even more important to track your money wisely. Every dollar counts. You cannot afford to let money slip through your fingers carelessly. You need the funds that would otherwise go toward fees to pay off your debts or reach your savings goals.

Why Should You Even Have a Budget?

Alright, let's talk about why having a budget is the MVP of adulting and break it down in a way we'll understand.

1. Having the Freedom to Spend Wisely
Imagine standing at a buffet with your favorite dishes laid out before you. Without a plan, you might pile your plate high with every option, only to find that you can't finish it all. That's how managing your money feels without a budget. A budget allows you to take control. You can look

at your expenses and decide which matter the most. You set your priorities. This means more fun experiences, like nights out with friends or a well-deserved vacation, are achievable when you know where your funds are going. Knowing your budget helps you feel empowered. You're not just reacting to bills; you're actively creating your spending path.

With a budget, you can see exactly how much money you can allocate toward discretionary spending. For example, if you've tracked your expenses and found that you consistently spend way too much on takeout, a budget can guide you to spend less in that area. That newfound freedom remains enjoyable because every dollar saved builds toward something greater (perhaps a trip that stretches your horizons or a new gadget that excites your passions). Let your budget be your financial map, charting a clear course through the fog of overspending and highlighting the endless possibilities along the way.

2. Gaining Peace of Mind
Picture yourself lying in bed, tossing and turning, with your mind racing with worries about the upcoming month. Will there be enough money to cover the rent? What if your car breaks down? These uncertainties can keep anyone up at night, eroding peace of mind. That's where a budget comes into play. A budget transforms uncertainty into certainty. When you know exactly how much you can spend and where your money will go, those midnight worries begin to fade.

Imagine planning a spontaneous weekend getaway. Instead of fretting about how it will affect your finances, you can confidently look at your budget. You see that there's some room for fun, and suddenly that last-minute adventure feels possible. Without a budget, you're left guessing. With a budget, you're prepared. Life's unpredictability won't be as frightening when you've mapped out a plan that accounts for both the expected costs and surprise expenses. You'll be able to enjoy life without a cloud of anxiety hanging over your head.

3. Achieving Your Goals
Do you have dreams that seem just out of reach? Whether it's owning a home, launching a business, or going back to school, these goals often appear daunting. However, a budget is your ally in making those aspirations a reality. With a structured financial plan, you can allocate specific amounts toward major milestones. For instance, if you dream of going back to school, setting aside money each month—whether it's $50 or $200—can make a world of difference over time.

When you see that slow but steady accumulation of savings, it transforms your mindset. You're not just dreaming; you're acting. One of my friends wanted to travel to Europe for years. After creating a budget, she identified her spending habits, cut unnecessary costs, and set a monthly savings target. Fast forward two years, and she was packing her bags for a trip she had always dreamed of. It wasn't magic; it was commitment and clarity from her budgeting efforts. Budgeting helps break down barriers. Your financial desires become tangible because you have a roadmap to follow.

4. Reducing Stress
Money stress affects countless people today. Bills pile up and unexpected expenses can feel like a heavy weight on your shoulders. Entering a shop for groceries shouldn't come with sweaty palms or anxiety. A budget alleviates that pressure. When you know exactly where your cash is allocated, you can confidently make decisions without the dread of overspending.

Consider the dread of shopping at the end of the month when your paycheck is dwindling. Without a budget, you might throw caution to the wind or stress over every item you put into your cart. With a budget, you know how much you can spend, allowing you to focus on making choices that bring joy without guilt. You're equipped to choose healthy options or treat yourself to a nice dessert without fear of negative financial repercussions. Budgeting brings a sense of calm. You become proactive rather than reactive, allowing you to handle life's uncertainties with grace.

5. Building Wealth
The journey begins with awareness and intention. A budget establishes both. Regular tracking of your income and expenses allows you to become aware of spending habits. From that observation, you can find areas where you can save. For example, have you noticed how your subscription services add up each month? Ending those unnecessary subscriptions and redirecting that cash toward savings or investments can make a significant difference over time.

As you start to save, even small amounts, consistently,

you cultivate a habit that leads to larger gains. Your budget becomes a foundational tool, propelling you toward financial independence. Once you acknowledge this, the discipline of saving and investing takes root. It might feel like a small effort now, but over years, that commitment can compound into true wealth. You're laying the groundwork for a secure and abundant future. It's not merely about getting by; it's about thriving. The benefits of a budget echo through every aspect of your financial journey, reinforcing the value of your money and improving your quality of life each step of the way.

The Fundamentals of a Budget

So, what should really go into a budget? There are five key elements to consider when creating a budget that works for you.

Income

Income is not just a number. It represents your hard work, your time, and your dedication. This is the fuel that powers your financial machine. Understanding what you bring in monthly is the first fundamental step in crafting a budget that serves you well. It can feel overwhelming as you look at your bills and obligations.

You're not alone if your income sometimes leaves you feeling drained and anxious. Let's put things into perspective and break down your income. Are you earning a steady salary? Or do you have a side hustle bringing in some extra cash? Have you been blessed with passive income from investments or rental properties?

Each source counts. Knowing your total monthly income helps you make informed choices.

For many millennials today, managing inconsistency in income can be challenging. Freelance work fluctuates, and some traditional jobs offer salaries that barely keep up with rising living costs. In those moments of uncertainty, it becomes imperative to create a financial structure that can support you. It doesn't mean you are stuck or defeated; it means you have the power to adapt and thrive. Tracking every dollar helps you see the big picture. Keep receipts. Use apps. Jot things down in a journal. Whatever helps you stay organized is where you should start.

Sometimes we underestimate how vital this awareness can be. For example, just knowing your monthly income can create a psychological shift. Imagine facing your expenses head-on instead of letting them loom in the background like a dark cloud. Awareness leads to empowerment. When you recognize your income streams, you become more confident. You can take action instead of reacting out of fear or uncertainty.

When budgeting, it's crucial to be realistic. If you expect a hefty paycheck one month from freelance work, don't let that set the standard. Average your income over several months. Factor in bonuses sparingly and never rely on them. Otherwise, you risk feeling like a sinking ship when they don't come through. Write down the trustworthy sources of income because they are your lifelines.

Now, many of us fall into the trap of living paycheck to paycheck because we feel pressured to meet societal standards. Your friends may seem leveled up with their lifestyles, but your path is unique. Don't be swayed by appearances. A budget allows you to take control and decide where your income goes.

Having your income identified is just the beginning. It's essential to celebrate every penny that comes your way but be solution-oriented. When you view income through a lens of gratitude rather than comparison, you unlock the potential to grow.

Expenses

As we shift our focus from income, let's shine a light on expenses. These are the everyday costs that eat away at your hard-earned money: rent, groceries, utilities, entertainment, and more. Understanding your expenses is crucial to creating a realistic budget. Think of it like this: Your income is the stream flowing into a pond, while your expenses are the holes in the pond's bottom through which the water drains. If the holes are too big, the pond goes dry, no matter how much water you pour in. Therefore, tracking your expenses is not just an exercise; it's necessary for financial survival.

Start by recording every penny you spend. Yes, every cent matters! Whether it's your weekly coffee run or that late-night takeaway, jot it all down. Use budgeting apps or a simple journal to keep track. When you accumulate this data, patterns will emerge. You may be surprised to find out how much those little expenses accumulate over time. For instance, spending $5 on coffee four times a week adds up to $80 a month. That's $960 a year. It's not about depriving yourself; it's about being informed. Bringing awareness to your spending habits allows you to make adjustments that align with your financial goals.

Consider your largest expenses first. Statistically, housing costs represent a significant portion of most millennials' budgets. If your rent is eating up more than 30% of your monthly income, it might be time to reevaluate your living situation. Are there cheaper alternatives available? Would a roommate help ease the burden? A friend of mine faced this dilemma. She was living alone in a pricey studio apartment. After doing some calculations and having a few conversations, she decided to move into a shared space. The result? Lower rent, less stress, and new friendships blooming in the process. Sometimes, change leads to unexpected blessings.

Utility bills cannot be overlooked. These essential payments can easily creep up if you're not cautious. Consider regularly checking your usage. Are you leaving lights on in empty rooms? Unplugging devices can provide additional savings. Every small action adds up and contributes to greater savings over time.

Let's talk about variable expenses too. How often do we underestimate our grocery bills? Meal planning can significantly help with this. By budgeting for groceries in advance, you can avoid impulse purchases and food waste. It took me a while to discover the magic of meal prepping. Preparing a week's worth of meals in one go not only saves cash but also time during a busy week.

You'll find yourself spending less and eating healthier.

Entertainment is another area where it's easy to overspend. Social outings and streaming subscriptions can sneak up on you. Have monthly movie nights instead of frequent dinners out. Look for free events in your community. Share experiences with friends rather than replacing them with expensive outings. This is about creativity, not deprivation.

Be mindful of the psychology behind spending. Are you spending money out of boredom or stress? Identify your triggers. If shopping gives you a temporary high but leaves you feeling guilty afterward, it's time for a shift. Channel that energy into experiences or personal development instead. Your worth is not tied to material possessions.

Savings and Investments

Too many people live paycheck to paycheck. They struggle just to keep their heads above water. Don't forget to pay yourself first! This simple, yet powerful, mantra can transform your relationship with money. It's not just about surviving; it's about thriving.

When I first began managing my finances, I thought saving was something I could do later. After all, bills needed to be paid, right? Wrong. I soon learned that if I didn't set aside money for savings, I was simply perpetuating a cycle of stress. It's like trying to fill a cup while there's a hole at the bottom. You'll never get ahead! To genuinely create financial security, you must treat your savings as a non-negotiable expense.

Start small. Aim to save 10% of your income initially. You may be thinking, How can I afford that? Let's be real. What's more daunting is the prospect of being financially unprepared during emergencies or retirement. Automate your savings if you need to. Set up a separate savings account. You won't miss the money if it goes to another account automatically.

Here's a practical approach: Every time you receive your paycheck, take a moment to create a "pay yourself first" line item. Let's say you make $3,000 a month. Transfer $300 into your savings account before you tackle your bills or indulge in anything else. This creates the habit of prioritizing your financial wellness. Over time, that money in your savings account will grow. Plus, watch how your mindset shifts when you see that balance increase. It's empowering.

Now let's shift gears to investments. Investing may feel intimidating, but it's nuanced. The sooner you start investing, the better for your future self. The goal here is to build wealth that works for you over time. This leads to financial freedom, which is God's intention for our lives (after all, He desires that we prosper).

Consider familiarizing yourself with the stock market or other investment vehicles. You don't have to be a financial guru. Start with what you know. If you're passionate about technology, maybe invest in tech stocks. Do your research. Understand the companies you're putting your money into. Robo-advisors make it easy for beginners. They automatically create an investment portfolio tailored to your risk tolerance. Investing isn't limited to stocks. Think real estate too. If you have the means, rental properties can be an incredible income source. They not only build equity, but they can also offer passive income.

Moreover, don't lose sight of the spiritual side of finances. The Bible teaches us the value of stewardship. When you save and invest, you're not just accumulating wealth. You're also preparing to give generously. Think of it as sowing seeds for God's kingdom. Being financially healthy enables you to help others who are struggling.

Emergency Fund

I want to highlight a critical component of your budget: an emergency fund. If you think about it, life is full of surprises, isn't it? Just when you think everything is going smoothly, an unexpected event throws your plans into a tailspin. Maybe it's a sudden job loss or an expensive car repair. It may feel like the sky is falling, and your financial stability is at risk. To anchor yourself in these turbulent times, having an emergency fund is essential. I'm here to tell you that a well-stocked emergency fund can be your lifeline.

So, how much should you aim to save? The rule of thumb is enough to cover three to six months' worth of living expenses. This may sound daunting, especially when you're juggling expenses. But starting small can make a big difference. If you spend $2,500 monthly, aim to save $7,500 to $15,000 for your emergency fund. This doesn't need to happen at once. Break it down into manageable chunks. To begin, you can set aside $50 from each paycheck for your emergency fund. Before long, you'll start to see a cushion forming, and that sense of security will become a game changer.

When I faced my own financial trials, I wished I had more than a couple of hundred dollars stashed away. Many years ago, my car unexpectedly broke down on a rainy afternoon. I felt the weight of stress creep in. However, because I had a small emergency fund, I could cover the repair without going into debt. This situation was a powerful reminder that planning pays off! Let me impress upon you that financial peace comes from preparation.

Being proactive about saving doesn't mean you're immune to life's surprises. It means you hold the power to respond when they happen. Think of your emergency fund as a safety net that allows you to bounce back faster. And let's not forget the psychological aspect. Research shows that having savings boosts your confidence and lowers anxiety. You're less likely to feel overwhelmed when you know you're prepared for hurdles.

If you're still scratching your head about how to save, consider setting up a dedicated savings account, which is separate from your everyday checking account. By automating the process, you'll make saving a priority and build your emergency fund without even thinking about it.

Debt Repayment

If you're carrying balances from student loans or credit cards, adding debt repayment to your budget is wise and essential for your financial health. I've been there, staring at bills piling up and feeling like a balloon slowly losing air. It can be overwhelming, but I want you to know you don't have to let debt define your story. Instead, you can take charge and write a new chapter.

So, how should you approach this? Create a clear plan. List all your debts, including the amounts owed and their interest rates. This transparency is empowering. You can see where you stand. While we've already discussed the strategies in the previous chapter, it's worth mentioning again.

Consider the snowball method. Focus on paying off the smallest debt first. Let's say you owe $500 on one credit card and $3,500 on another. Pour all your extra money into paying off the $500 balance. Once that debt is gone, tackle the next smallest debt. It can be a liberating experience. The psychological boost is powerful.

You can also try the avalanche method. This involves prioritizing debts based on interest rates. Pay off the debt with the highest interest first to save money in the long run. For instance, if you have a credit card charging 18% interest, knock that out before focusing on a student loan at 5%. You'll end up paying less interest. It's like finding hidden treasure. Choosing the right approach is key, depending on whether you thrive on small victories or need to minimize interest costs.

While you're repaying debts, consider adjusting your spending. Identify areas where you can cut back. This might be as simple as dining out less or canceling an unused subscription service. Use these savings to tackle your debts faster. Every dollar counts. Being consistent will build momentum on your journey.

Let's Create a Budget Together

Now that we've explored the importance of debt repayment, it's time to integrate that knowledge into a robust budgeting strategy. Creating a budget is like drafting a financial roadmap. With each line you draw, you define your path to financial peace. Embrace this process because a well-structured budget is your ally in overcoming debt and achieving your goals.

So, where do you begin? Start by assessing your monthly income. Make a list or use budgeting software. Include all sources of income, from your salary to side hustles. Look at your total monthly earnings, then subtract your essential expenses—think rent or mortgage, utilities, and groceries. This figure will give you insight into your discretionary spending and, more crucially, your debt repayment capacity.

Next, itemize your debts. Write down each one. Include the amount owed, minimum payments, and interest rates. Seeing everything laid out helps clarify your situation. It takes away the fog of uncertainty. This transparency is crucial. Each month, dedicate a portion of your income toward your debts. But don't forget your emergency fund. Balancing these two priorities may feel daunting, but it is essential for long-term financial health.

When creating your budget, consider using the 50/30/20 rule. Allocate 50% of your income to needs, 30% to wants, and set aside 20% for savings and debt repayment. This strategy ensures you're meeting your essential expenses while actively tackling your debt. Flipping the script on what it means to spend can change your perspective. It shifts your focus from merely surviving to thriving. You set yourself up for financial success.

Let's break it down further. In a month, say your income is $3,000. According to this rule:
- $1,500 for needs: rent or mortgage, groceries, and transportation
- $900 for wants: eating out, subscriptions, and entertainment
- $600 for savings and debt repayment: Your priority should be funding your emergency fund first. Once you have a solid foundation, channel more toward aggressive debt repayment.

As you allocate your funds, keep an eye on your progress. Celebrate small victories. Each time you pay off a debt, it's a reminder of your strength. With every dollar, you're one step closer to financial freedom. Track your journey. Gamifying this experience can keep you engaged, so use charts, graphs, or even a debt countdown.

A critical piece of wisdom from the Bible applies here. Proverbs 21:5 tells us, "The plans of the diligent lead to profit as surely as haste leads to poverty." Approach your budgeting with diligence. Spend time crafting your plan.

Don't rush through it. Let it evolve as you do.

Remember what I experienced during my financial struggles. I faced anxiety every time bills arrived, but I committed myself to a budget. I created a list each payday and felt empowered as I crossed off debts. This simple act shifted my mindset. I began to see myself as a conqueror, not a victim.

EXPERT HIGHLIGHT
Tamekia Fallin

Senior Marketing Director
Author I Speaker I Community Leader I Event Host
World System Builder/World Financial Group
Website: www.tamekiafallin.com
Email Address: stepstofinancialwealth@gmail.com
Podcast: Sister Friend Talks

Meet Tamekia Fallin

Tamekia Fallin is a dynamic leader and passionate advocate for financial empowerment. With a career spanning diverse industries—including Government IT Contracting, where she held a Top Secret Clearance, and managing Telesales and Customer Service departments—Tamekia ultimately found her true calling in the financial industry as a Financial Professional and Educator.

Her transformative journey began with her introduction to WFG/WSB, a leading financial literacy organization. Immersed in world-class training, Tamekia mastered key concepts and tools in personal finance, fundamentally transforming her financial future.

Today, Tamekia is on a mission to share this life-changing knowledge across North America. She empowers individuals to build strong financial foundations and take control of their financial destinies. Tamekia passionately believes that financial security is the great equalizer, and that personal transformation is the first step toward a better world.

Through education and empowerment, Tamekia Fallin is paving the way for brighter financial futures for individuals and communities alike.

Personal Financial Mindset

Question: How can someone begin shifting from a scarcity mindset to an abundance mindset regarding their finances?

The first step toward transformation is making a firm decision to change. True change cannot happen if you are still in love with your current habits, lifestyle, or self-image. Growth requires commitment; wavering between wanting change and staying comfortable leads to stagnation. Life will not shift for you while you are sitting on the fence—you must take action.

Once you commit to shifting from a scarcity mindset to an abundance mindset, the following steps are essential:

Identify Limiting Beliefs:
Write down the negative thoughts or internalized beliefs you hold about money.
Example: "I will never have enough money."

Reframe Your Thinking:
Replace limiting beliefs with positive, empowering affirmations.
Example: "I have the ability to attract and grow wealth."

Focus on Abundance:
Practice gratitude daily, no matter how small the wins. Train your mind to recognize opportunities instead of focusing on lack.

Invest in Yourself:
Commit to learning more about personal finance, investing, and wealth-building strategies. Utilize books, podcasts, courses, and videos to continue growing.

Surround Yourself with Growth-Minded Individuals:
Build relationships with people who have achieved the success you seek or who can mentor and inspire you to expand your thinking and habits.

Budgeting Basics

Question: Why is it essential to have a budget, even if you feel like you're living paycheck to paycheck?

While this may be difficult for some to hear, many people live paycheck to paycheck simply because they do not have a budget. A budget is not just about restriction—it's a strategic financial tool that helps you track your income, control your spending, and allocate resources intentionally to meet your financial goals. Your budget becomes the foundation for financial success.

Over the years, working with individuals from all walks of life, I have seen that many either do not have a budget or fail to consistently use one. As the saying goes, "People don't plan to fail; they fail to plan."

Often, when clients finally sit down with a financial professional, they are amazed to discover hundreds—or even thousands—of dollars they were unknowingly wasting each month. By implementing a budget, they uncover hidden resources they can redirect toward savings, debt repayment, and wealth-building.

Overcoming Financial Challenges

Question: What steps should someone take if they've never budgeted before and feel overwhelmed by the process? What advice would you give to those struggling with credit card debt or student loans while trying to budget?

If the thought of budgeting feels overwhelming, start with these key actions:

> ***Get a Financial Coach:***
> Just like athletes need coaches to win championships, you need guidance for financial success. A financial professional can help you create a personalized plan, hold you accountable, and monitor your progress.
>
> ***Automate and Simplify:***
> Automate your bill payments and savings contributions to stay consistent without daily stress.
>
> ***Start Small:***
> Focus on one area at a time. For example, commit to eating out less. Set SMART goals—Specific, Measurable, Achievable, Relevant, and Time-bound.
>
> ***Track Spending for 30 Days:***
> Use apps, spreadsheets, or even the envelope

system to track where every dollar goes.

Celebrate Small Wins:
Acknowledging your progress, no matter how minor, builds momentum and strengthens your winning mindset.

Every budget should also include a debt management strategy. If you are struggling with credit card debt or student loans, understand that discipline and consistency are crucial. Unless your income is truly insufficient to meet your basic needs, overcoming debt is typically a matter of restructuring habits.

If income is an issue, consider the following options:
- Increase your income through side jobs or career advancement.
- Reduce or eliminate unnecessary expenses.
- Negotiate terms with your creditors.
- Consolidate debts where appropriate.
- Utilize balance transfers to lower-interest credit cards.
- Apply unexpected income (bonuses, tax refunds) strategically toward debt.
- Consider bankruptcy only as an absolute last resort.

Tamekia Fallin's Closing Advice on Budgeting

Budgeting is about empowerment—taking control of your finances and making your money work for you. It's not about denying yourself joy or opportunity; it's about creating a clear, strategic path toward your goals and the lifestyle you desire.

Start small. Track your spending. Be flexible and give yourself grace when mistakes happen. Keep your goals front and center. Seek out professional guidance and use available tools and resources to simplify the process. Over time, budgeting will become a natural habit, and you will begin to design the life you choose to live—on your terms.

Chapter 3
Money & Marriage

Over the years, I started to advance in my career. I worked hard and gained recognition. However, my salary was not enough to make ends meet. This created stress in my life and my marriage. Financial strain often feels heavy and can create tension between spouses. I noticed how it affected the communication and intimacy between me and my husband.

The more intimate my relationship with God became, the more I noticed Him revealing truths to me. In the Bible, we see the importance of handling finances wisely. Proverbs 21:20 says, "The wise store up choice food and olive oil, but fools gulp theirs down." This verse reminds us to be careful with our resources. Wise decisions lead to stability in our homes.

The enemy seeks to keep married couples in financial bondage. This is a strategy to cause division. Financial troubles can lead to mistrust and frustration. Many couples argue about money. They may feel trapped in a cycle of debt and scarcity. It can feel impossible to break free, so this is where faith plays a vital role. Relying on God can bring peace amidst financial chaos.

In this chapter, I'll go into more detail about the impact of money and other things on a marriage and how couples can overcome financial struggles together. I'll also share practical tips for managing finances and communicating effectively with your spouse about money matters. Remember, God wants us to thrive in every aspect of our lives, including our finances and marriages. Let's dive in and see how we can build a stronger foundation for both.

Communication, Problems & Infidelity

Let's deep dive into the connection between money and the top three causes of divorce: communication, financial issues, and infidelity. I understand the trauma that a lack of communication can bring into a marriage. Without open, honest discussions, couples can find themselves in a dark place. Communication is not just about sharing words; it is about sharing feelings and concerns.

One of the inspirations for this book is to emphasize how financial hardships impacted my marriage among a host of other factors and how they connect to the three major causes of divorce: financial issues, poor communication, and infidelity. We entered marriage already burdened by financial strain, and without the tools to communicate effectively, we found ourselves spiraling. This ultimately led to two divorce filings and painful experiences of broken trust. Even in this, I thank God for every mountain He brought me over, because through it all, I gained life's lessons and experiences to help other people.

If a husband and wife do not talk about their schedules, routines, and financial troubles, things can go downhill quickly. This scenario can lead to frustration and misunderstandings. It is like taking a trip down a dead-end road. In relationships, a lack of communication about finances can breed confusion and resentment. If one partner is not financially savvy or is unwilling to discuss financial issues, it can create significant conflict. Arguments can arise, confusion can fill the household, and trust can erode the relationship.

When you are married, it is essential to be on the same page as your spouse regarding finances. You both need to agree on your financial plans and budget as a team. Communication is key here. My husband and I faced our challenges head-on one night after putting the children to bed. We sat down at the kitchen table for a heart-to-heart conversation. We discussed all our debts and the heavy loads we had been carrying.

Before that night, I found it hard to talk about finances. Conversations about money often led to finger-pointing or heated arguments. However, that night was different. We were exhausted by our money problems. We were fed up. This time, the conversation felt peaceful. It was a breakthrough for us. We agreed to tackle our issues together, which helped strengthen our bond.

I must say that Jesus was present when my husband and I had our essential conversation about finances. Before I became saved, discussions about money were often approached with sarcasm. They were filled with frustration and anger. This time was different. I stepped aside and allowed God to lead the meeting.

My husband placed some paper and a pencil on the table, and we decided to take a traditional approach to creating our budget. We worked together. First, we both listed our salaries. Then, we wrote down our current bills and acknowledged our mountains of debt. This process opened the door for meaningful dialogue. Finally, we were able to communicate effectively about our budget.

After that night, a weight was lifted off my shoulders.

Talking about finances with my spouse was a relief. It is not God's will for us to face our burdens alone. Carrying those loads leads to frustration. God created both male and female for connection and partnership. We are meant to build a beautiful marriage TOGETHER.

In the beginning, God desired for Adam and Eve to thrive together. They were meant to multiply and flourish. We cannot achieve multiplication without communication. Multiplication refers to efforts in all positive areas in our lives. This includes the Kingdom of God. God wants us to experience abundance in our work efforts, especially when we come together in holy matrimony.

Then God said, 'Let us make mankind in our image, in our likeness, so that they may rule over the fish in the sea and the birds in the sky, over the livestock and all the wild animals, and over all the creatures that move along the ground.' So, God created mankind in his own image, in the image of God he created them; male and female he created them.

God blessed them and said to them, 'Be fruitful and increase in number; fill the earth and subdue it. Rule over the fish in the sea and the birds in the sky and over every living creature that moves on the ground.' Then God said, "I give you every seed-bearing plant on the face of the whole earth and every tree that has fruit with seed in it. They will be yours for food." (Genesis 1:26-29)

A lack of communication, combined with financial issues, can lead to a dark path that may involve infidelity. Spouses might seek comfort outside their marriage. They may share their financial and marital struggles with someone else. This can create distance and distrust in a relationship.

After a long workday, I often feel drained. I do not want to talk about bills or finances. However, these conversations are crucial. If you delay talking about finances, things can worsen. Spending quality time with your spouse is essential because it helps you find solutions together. The longer you put off talking, the longer it will take for God to move your mountains.

At the beginning of our marriage, my husband and I received two prophetic words. We were told we would never have to worry about money. The prophets saw "business, business, business" written over me. It felt encouraging, but the prosperity gospel can be very confusing. Many people do not have a personal relationship with God. I assumed a miracle would simply happen. I hoped for a check to arrive in the mail. I thought that money would just fall from the sky. But that is not how God works.

If you want to receive God's blessings, you must put in the work. You need to be active in seeking financial wisdom. You and your spouse must manage your finances together as a couple. Money will not simply come to you. You have to fight for financial freedom. Both partners must be willing to communicate openly and often. This commitment will help build a stronger foundation for your marriage.

James 2:26 says, "For as the body without the spirit is

dead, so faith without works is dead also." This verse highlights an important truth. If you want to see changes in your life, you cannot have faith alone. You must also put in the actual work. God shows us visions of what He wants for us. However, He often does not reveal the steps we must take to reach those goals.

I was determined to allow God to help me overcome the burden of debt. I wanted to create a better life for my family, so I knew I had to be obedient to His guidance. As I embraced this journey, God began to work miracle after miracle in my family. It started with my children being blessed in ways we had not expected. My husband and I received promotions and raises at our jobs. Incredible new doors opened for us. These changes were just the beginning.

God wants your marriage to be filled with blessings. He does not want you to feel broke or burdened. Unity in your relationship is essential. It is not God's plan for couples to work against each other. When I said "yes" to God, everything shifted. I dedicated my life to Christ and built a strong relationship with Him. This commitment opened many doors. I began to receive divine connections and plans that guided me through my challenges. They also led me to the blessings that helped move my mountains.

Even while I worked on my family's finances, I saw God's presence in my husband's actions. Our communication really began to improve. We understood that to see our mountains move, we needed to partner together as husband and wife.

One night, my husband and I decided to discuss our financial situation. After sharing my struggles, he looked at me and said, "Wow! I can't believe you've been dealing with all of this on your own. I am surprised you still have hair on your head." His comment made me laugh. It showed me how much I had bottled up. I had been carrying all the financial stress myself. Meanwhile, I knew he was dealing with his own challenges too.

This experience taught me a valuable lesson. I encourage all married couples to step back and let God guide their conversations about finances. Let Him lead you both as you discuss these important topics with one another. He will provide wisdom and direction. When you include God, the conversation changes.

The 3 Golden Rules of Communication

I have learned that effective communication is crucial in a marriage, especially regarding finances. Managing money is not just a mere transaction; it flows into every corner of our lives, influencing our dreams, fears, and future plans. On our journey, my husband and I discovered three golden rules that transformed our conversations about money and, consequently, our relationship.

1. Always be respectful to one another. Respect is the bedrock of any healthy conversation. When discussing finances, it's easy to let frustration seep into the dialogue, especially when disagreements arise. I vividly remember a late-night talk where my husband expressed his concerns about our budget. It would have been easy to dismiss his feelings. Instead, I took a

deep breath and listened. Respect does not just mean being polite. It involves actively valuing each other's thoughts and emotions. When my husband felt heard, it opened the door for deeper understanding between us. We began to approach our discussions as a team.

2. Be open-minded. We are often set in our ways. I once believed that I had to manage my household's finances alone. It was a heavy burden I chose to carry. However, being open-minded means embracing new ideas and perspectives. I started to value my husband's contributions. In one meeting, he suggested using a shared app to track our expenses together. Initially, I was hesitant but trying it out changed everything. We had fun tracking our spending, and it became a bonding experience for us. Openness built collaboration during this time, and we began to see money not as a source of tension but as an area where we could grow together.

3. Prioritize communicating. It sounds simple, but prioritizing communication is often relegated to the back burner. Many couples wait until financial crises arise to have a discussion about money. Don't wait. Create a space for regular conversations about your finances. My husband and I established a weekly "money date." During this time, we shared our thoughts without distractions. We laughed, brainstormed, and tackled issues together. This routine has led to greater clarity and trust. Regular check-ins have made us feel like partners in our financial future.

As we embrace these three golden rules of communication, it's essential to remember the wisdom found in Colossians 3:12-17: "Therefore, as God's chosen people, holy and dearly loved, clothe yourselves with compassion, kindness, humility, gentleness and patience. Bear with each other and forgive one another if any of you has a grievance against someone. Forgive as the Lord forgave you. And over all these virtues put on love, which binds them all together in perfect unity. Let the peace of Christ rule in your hearts, since as members of one body you were called to peace. And be thankful. Let the message of Christ dwell among you richly as you teach and admonish one another with all wisdom through psalms, hymns, and songs from the Spirit, singing to God with gratitude in your hearts. And whatever you do, whether in word or deed, do it all in the name of the Lord Jesus, giving thanks to God the Father through him."

By integrating these rules into our marriage, and with God's guidance, communication between me and my husband flourished. We gained not only financial footing but also a strong spiritual connection. The conversation about money shifted from resentment to collaboration. This experience taught us that even the toughest topics can turn into stepping stones toward a brighter future when God is at the center. Remember, financial discussions do not have to be daunting. When approached with love and intentionality, they can become a powerful tool for wealth—both spiritually and financially.

Planning the Right Way

1. Set Financial Goals Together
Setting financial goals with your spouse is a crucial step in any marriage. It's like planning a journey. You wouldn't set off on a road trip without a map or a destination in mind, would you? That's why it's essential to have open conversations about your financial dreams and targets. Sit down with your spouse, perhaps over a cup of your favorite drink, and brainstorm what matters most to each of you. Do you envision living in a cozy home, saving for a child's education, or going on vacation to an exotic location?

Proverbs 15:22 reminds us that "plans fail for lack of counsel, but with many advisers they succeed." Don't hesitate to seek advice from trusted friends or financial advisors. It's valuable to bounce ideas off each other. My husband and I were once advised to pick one day out of the week to sit down and reflect on our financial situation. During these weekly sessions, we went over our bills, discussed our weeks, and asked how we could support each other. If you have children, consider making this part of their bedtime routine. It can be a calm ending to a busy day while instilling financial awareness in your kids.

When you and your spouse set goals together, it not only aligns your financial aspirations but deepens your connection as partners. Think about dividing long-term goals into short-term milestones. For instance, if your ultimate goal is to buy a house, perhaps your first step is saving for a down payment. Make it tangible and rewarding. Celebrate small victories, whether that's reaching a specific savings target or sticking to a budget for one month.

Reflect on the past year. Where did your money go? How much did you spend on entertainment, dining out, or even impulse purchases? Such reflections help identify patterns and areas where you might be able to cut back. You are creating a shared vision that will serve as a guiding light during challenges. Discussions about money do not have to be confrontational.

2. Talk about Money Regularly
Conversations about money can be tough, but they're necessary. Just reflecting on my past experiences makes me remember how hesitant I used to feel to talk about finances. My palms would sweat, and I'd find every excuse to avoid the conversation. Yet, I quickly learned that stepping into that discomfort was where growth really happened. Once I mustered the courage to sit with my husband, I felt like I was shedding a weight I didn't even know I was carrying. Hallelujah! This openness became a pivotal moment for us, and there's a good reason for it.

Ephesians 4:15 encourages us to "speak the truth in love." It's vital to approach financial discussions in a way that feels safe and loving. Start by sharing your worries, dreams, and financial realities openly. This could look like sitting down together with your financial statements sprawled out on the kitchen table or cozying up on the couch with a notebook. Maybe start by talking about lighter topics first. What's been a recent win in your finances? It can be empowering to celebrate those small victories. When you create a space where the both of you feel comfortable, it opens the door to vulnerability and deeper understanding.

You don't have to have financial discussions every day, but you can make doing so part of your routine. Aim to set a designated time each week—maybe every Sunday afternoon after church. That's your time to reflect together. Review your expenses, discuss any impulsive purchases, and brainstorm ways to support each other in reaching your financial goals. This consistency is key because it fosters a habit of open communication, reducing anxiety around money matters. Practicing this strategy allowed me and my husband to stay aligned and aware of each other's feelings toward our finances.

When it feels right, dive deeper. Talk about future goals and what you both need to do to achieve them. Don't underestimate the power of listening. Sometimes, just letting your spouse voice their struggles is more meaningful than jumping straight to finding solutions.

3. Budget Like a Team

Budgeting isn't merely about numbers and restrictions. It's about creating a shared vision for your financial future. Proverbs 21:5 reminds us that "The plans of the diligent lead surely to abundance, but everyone who is hasty comes only to poverty." This wisdom couldn't hold more truth for couples navigating their finances. Picture this: You and your spouse are sitting together, papers spread out on a table, with your favorite snacks in hand. In that moment, you are not just crunching numbers;

you are crafting your financial game plan.

Begin with an honest assessment of your income and expenses. What do you bring in every month? Are there expenses you can reduce or eliminate? Consider using budgeting apps or spreadsheets that track your spending habits. These tools can help you stay accountable. For instance, if you notice excessive spending on dining out, challenge yourselves to cook more meals at home. Not only will this save money, but it will also become an opportunity for you two to quality time together. Turning cooking into a fun date night can change your perspective on budgeting altogether.

Set clear, achievable goals. Maybe you want to save for a family vacation or eliminate debt. Break these goals down into manageable steps. Just as you wouldn't expect to save for a vacation overnight, don't pressure yourselves to cut everything out at once. Let's say you aim to save $1,200 for a vacation. Rather than skimming your budget down to zero, start saving $100 a month. Celebrate those initial victories! When you reach a milestone, reward yourselves. Maybe go out for a special dinner or on a weekend getaway. This way, budgeting becomes an exciting journey you two share together.

Discuss your budget periodically. I remember when my husband and I first started this routine. It felt cumbersome at first. However, as we became comfortable with our sit-downs, we began diving deeper into our finances and aspirations. We transitioned from just tracking numbers to discussing our dreams and fears. Maybe you worry about retirement or wonder how your lifestyle choices will impact your children's futures. Lay those possibilities on the table.

Be patient and thorough. Financial discussions can feel daunting, but they are necessary for growth. Progress requires time and commitment, but when you look back, you'll see how far you've come together financially and in your relationship. And therein lies the beauty of budgeting as a team; it brings you closer to each other while propelling you toward financial freedom.

4. Live Within Your Means
In a world obsessed with keeping up appearances, it's easy to overspend. I know this from experience. At one point, my life mimicked a race where everyone else seemed to have better cars, fancier clothes, and chic vacations. The pressure was overwhelming, and I fell for it hook, line, and sinker. Then, the fog of debt enveloped me. Proverbs 22:7 reminds us that "The rich rules over the poor, and the borrower is the slave of the lender." Those words resonate deeply when you feel the weight of their truth.

Living within your means is not just about restraint; it's about finding joy in simplicity. It's about realizing that it's perfectly okay to choose a cozy night in over an extravagant dinner out. I remember my husband and I starting a 'staycation' tradition. Instead of booking an expensive getaway, we planned special evenings at home. We'd cook a nice meal together and take time to reminisce about the past. Those evenings were golden, and they didn't require extra dollars to enjoy.

Identify the difference between needs and wants. Ask yourself if that shiny gadget or trendy outfit you've been eyeing truly adds value to your life or merely boosts your social standing. I've found that writing down my expenses helped clarify what was essential. For instance, do you need that daily latte? Consider brewing your morning coffee at home and using those savings to treat yourself once a month instead.

Embrace contentment. When you focus on gratitude, you start appreciating what you have. Maybe you have a reliable car instead of the latest model. Rejoice in the fact that your vehicle gets you where you need to go. Many Christians turn to God's teachings when facing financial dilemmas. Trust in His provision. Embark on your spending journey with prayer and ask for wisdom as you navigate making different choices. Engaging with your faith can provide comfort and clarity during challenging times.

Creating this discipline won't happen overnight. It requires commitment. It may mean letting go of plans with friends occasionally to stick to your financial goals. I'll admit, those first sacrifices felt daunting. Yet, with each small choice, the burden began to lift. The brighter days approached as I regained control over my finances. This is not a lonely path. Your spouse is your partner here, so share the journey and tackle it together.

5. *Save and Invest Wisely*
Planning for the future is all about exercising wisdom. As I reflect on my financial journey, I can't emphasize enough how crucial it is to save and invest wisely.

Proverbs 21:20 tells us, "The wise store up choice food and olive oil, but fools gulp theirs down." This wisdom can be applied to our finances too. When you save, you're essentially preparing for leaner times and paving the way for brighter days ahead.

Starting small is often the key. You don't need to cushion your savings account with large amounts right away. Even setting aside a modest sum each month can snowball into a significant safety net. My grandma used to say, "Look after the pennies, and the pounds will look after themselves." It's a simple concept but an effective one. She would say even if it's $5 a week, it adds up.

You want to make sure you put your saved funds to work by investing in low-risk opportunities. Seek advice from a financial advisor or research reputable investment options. As Christians, we are called to be good stewards of our resources. Don't fall into the trap of get-rich-quick schemes or risky investments that may compromise your values. Trust in God's timing and guidance as you make wise decisions for your future.

When you focus on these principles of saving and investing wisely, you prepare a solid foundation for your future. Financial freedom begins with small steps that lead to big changes. With each decision, you are cultivating a lifestyle filled with intentionality. You are creating a narrative where your financial goals harmonize with God's purpose for you.

6. Give Generously
Giving isn't just about money; it's about making a

difference. As Malachi 3:10 encourages us, "'Bring the whole tithe into the storehouse, that there may be food in my house. Test me in this,' says the Lord Almighty, 'and see if I will not throw open the floodgates of heaven and pour out so much blessing that there will not be room enough to store it.'" This verse resonates deeply with me because it encapsulates a promise from God that there is divine reciprocity when we give. There will be more on this in the next chapter.

Understanding that generosity is a reflection of God's love is significant. It seriously reshapes how we should approach finances. It's easy to feel overwhelmed by financial challenges. Yet, when you step outside of your struggles and focus on how you can help others, it changes the narrative. When we give joyfully, we don't just lift the burdens of those around us; we also lighten the load of our own worries. This creates a cycle of gratitude that deepens faith in God's provision and in our shared community.

Many times, I have seen how communities uplift one another through acts of generosity. Whether it's a meal for a neighbor who lost a job or helping a friend pay for unexpected expenses, those gestures leave lasting impacts. They help build a supportive network where everyone feels valued. One small act can ignite a sense of hope in someone else and instill motivation to pay it forward.

As we explore how to give generously in the next chapter, let's ensure we keep our hearts open. Challenge yourself to identify causes that resonate with you. It could be anything from supporting a local charity to volunteering at a community center. No act is too small, and every contribution matters.

7. Learn and Grow Together
Financial education is crucial for any couple wanting to thrive together. Proverbs 19:20 reminds us to listen to advice and accept discipline.

Take courses, read books, or attend financial seminars with your spouse. As a certified credit union financial counselor, I run into situations where only one spouse actively works on the finances while the other spouse doesn't have any interest or motivation to move upward and forward to be in a better financial position. If that is the position you are in now, pray for your spouse. Ask God to give them the actionable spirit to get up off the couch to stop delaying and procrastinating. Pray that God will give your partner the spirit to create solutions.

If you are the spouse that has the desire to move, then keep moving. Do not let your husband or wife's lack of mobility stop or block your motivation. Truthfully, sometimes both individuals will not have the same skill sets, tools, knowledge, or entrepreneurial spirit to move the needle forward. But you cannot stay in lack. Keep going. Pray for your spouse. As things work out, you will be able to inspire them and provide guidance in no time.

I am always trying to increase my faith and knowledge. I serve a loving God and am not going to be complacent. I am going to move so that God can move. God can't bless what we won't do. Once you are at the point where your spouse will engage, invest in your financial knowledge as a couple. You'll be better equipped to handle whatever life throws your way.

So, always remember that one and one make eleven. That's the concept of teamwork. When you work together, the synergy that comes from unity is unstoppable. Combining your individual strengths and talents allows you to overcome any obstacles in your financial journey. Learning and growing together not only strengthens your relationship, but it also empowers you to reach your goals with greater ease.

Marriage is a beautiful gift from God. It is a unique bond that should be nurtured and cherished. By applying these biblical principles to your finances, you are laying the foundation for a strong, flourishing marriage that honors God's purpose for your lives together. And as a by-product, this makes you both financially sound for generations to come.

EXPERT HIGHLIGHT
Pastor Odell Cleveland

Retired Chief Administrative Officer Mount Zion Baptist Church Greensboro, NC
Author I Speaker I Leader I Personality
Website: www.odellcleveland.com
Podcast: P is for Prostate
Bill & ODell Finding Common Ground

Meet Pastor Odell Cleveland

Rev. Odell Cleveland is a trailblazing leader, visionary, and advocate for community empowerment. In 2022, he was one of only 12 individuals nationwide to receive AARP's Local Hero's Award for his exceptional caregiving leadership. His impact extends far beyond recognition, as evidenced by his role in the White House COVID-19 Virtual Roundtable for NC Leaders in 2021.

As the founder of America's first faith-based community action agency, the Welfare Reform Liaison Project (WRLP), Rev. Cleveland transformed a small annex of Mount Zion Baptist Church into a $100 million nonprofit organization, profoundly influencing the lives of North Carolina's most vulnerable communities. Today, he continues his leadership as Chief Administrative Officer of Greensboro's 7,000-member Mount Zion Baptist Church.

Rev. Cleveland is also a compelling voice in the public discourse. He co-hosts two podcasts: *P is for Prostate*, which addresses health and wellness, and *Bill & Odell: Finding Common Ground*, a platform that tackles racial divisions through meaningful dialogue.

A prolific speaker and author, Rev. Cleveland co-wrote *Pracademics and Community Change*, a seminal work on nonprofit development and social entrepreneurship. He uses his vast experience to connect communities, guide public leaders, and inspire transformative change rooted in shared values.

Rev. Cleveland holds a Master's in Divinity with honors from

Hood Theological Seminary and a B.S. in Management from the University of South Carolina at Spartanburg. Whether shaping nonprofit strategies, advocating for health and equity, or fostering unity through faith, Rev. Odell Cleveland exemplifies servant leadership with a vision for lasting impact.

Financial Communication in Marriage

Question: What are the most important financial conversations couples should have before and after marriage?

Understanding Different Perspectives on Money
The most important thing to understand is that people view money differently based on their backgrounds. For example, I grew up "city poor," living in urban areas with limited resources. My wife, on the other hand, was "country poor," growing up in rural areas. These experiences shaped how each of us approached money. It's essential to recognize that money is a tool—something to use wisely—not a toy for indulging whims.

Couples need to acknowledge that not everyone is good with money. Early in our marriage, my wife and I had to decide who would manage our finances. Her grandmother, who raised her, gave us simple but powerful advice: "If you can, pool your money together and work as a team." This approach may not suit everyone, but for us, it made a world of difference. By combining our resources, we could set common goals and hold each other accountable.

The Importance of Pre-Marriage Conversations
Before marriage, couples should discuss how they view and handle money. Some people don't understand the importance of saving, while others might spend excessively to impress others. These differences can lead to conflict if not addressed early. It's critical to talk about financial priorities, set boundaries, and agree on a system for managing money together.

Navigating Changing Dynamics After Marriage
Marriage doesn't stop at planning; the dynamics of money often shift during the relationship. One major challenge is when one spouse starts earning significantly more than the other, particularly if the wife becomes the higher earner. This situation can create tension, especially if the husband feels his role is diminished.

The key is understanding that marriage is a partnership. If all the money supports the household, it doesn't matter who earns more. Whoever has the "hot hand" at the time should be supported. As a husband, that might mean taking on additional responsibilities at home, like starting the laundry, washing dishes, or picking up the kids. Supporting your spouse's career doesn't make you less of a man—it strengthens your bond and helps the family succeed.

Practical Communication and Support
Successful couples regularly communicate about their schedules and responsibilities. A conversation as simple as, "Honey, what's your week like?" can lead to a game plan for handling work and home life. If your spouse has late meetings or deadlines, step in to ease the burden. Success in a professional career often requires as much preparation outside the office as it does during working hours.

Avoiding Money-Driven Conflict
Finally, one of the saddest stories I've heard involved a woman who didn't want to tell her husband about her large Christmas bonus because it always led to arguments—her bonus was larger than his. To me, that's absurd. Financial wins, regardless of whose name is on the paycheck, are wins for the family. Instead of competing with your spouse,

celebrate their successes and work together to build a strong financial foundation.

By discussing financial values early, adapting to changes during the marriage, and supporting each other's strengths, couples can navigate the complexities of money in marriage with unity *and grace.*

Faith and Financial Principles

Question: How has faith played a role in your financial journey, and what biblical principles guide your money decisions?

Faith as the Foundation

The central biblical principle that guides my financial journey is tithing. We believe in tithing to the church, but our giving extends beyond that. We've always felt that we are blessed to be a blessing, and that belief shapes how we approach our finances.

Both my wife and I came from humble beginnings, and giving was a part of our upbringing. My wife's grandmother, for example, would take whatever extra she had—whether it was food or other resources—and have my wife, as a child, deliver it to someone in need. It might be a bag of food or some fish, but those small acts of generosity made a big impact. That's the kind of community we grew up in—sharing what little we had with each other.

When we take those lessons and frame them within a biblical perspective, tithing and offering naturally become a priority. But for us, tithing isn't limited to the church. It's about recognizing need wherever we see it and acting on it.

The Tradition of "Blessing Money"
One of our family traditions is something we call "blessing money," and it's especially meaningful around the Christmas season. My wife started this tradition years ago, and it has grown to include our children and now even our grandchildren. Here's how it works: Each of us takes $20 or $30, and we use it to bless someone in need. It might be a homeless person, a waiter at a restaurant, or simply someone who our spirit leads us to help.

The beauty of blessing money is that it teaches the principle of giving. At the end of the season, we gather as a family and share how we used our blessing money. This reflection not only reinforces the value of generosity but also allows us to celebrate the impact of those small, thoughtful acts.

Teaching Generosity
One thing I've learned is that you have to teach people how to give. Receiving often comes naturally, but giving is a discipline that requires intentionality. In our family, we prioritize teaching this principle. Everyone understands what blessing money means—it's a reminder that we're stewards of the blessings we've received, and it's our responsibility to pass them on.

Gratitude for Growth
We started out dirt poor, but by God's grace, we're now in a position to do well by many standards. Yet, we never forget where we came from or the biblical call to give. Faith has not only shaped our financial decisions but has also created a legacy of generosity in our family.

As I often say, we're blessed to be a blessing, and it's a

privilege to live that out in every season of life.

Overcoming Financial Challenges in Marriage

Question: What was the most difficult financial challenge you faced in your marriage, and how did you overcome it together?

The Challenge of Credit Card Debt
One of the most difficult financial challenges we faced early in our marriage was dealing with credit cards. Like many young couples, we didn't fully understand how credit worked. We fell into the trap of transferring debt balances from one card to another, thinking it was a good way to manage our finances. At first, it seemed like a relief—moving from a higher interest rate to a lower one—but we didn't realize how dangerous it could be.

The real trap lies in the fine print. If you make a late payment, those low promotional interest rates can skyrocket to double figures, leaving you with a mountain of debt that's hard to climb out of. Young couples need to be cautious and avoid relying on credit cards as a financial crutch.

Managing Expectations
Another lesson we learned was the importance of managing expectations when it comes to lifestyle. As a young family, it's tempting to want everything brand new, especially when it comes to things like furniture or household items. But we realized it's okay to start with used items or hand-me-downs. Everything doesn't have to be shiny and new right away.

Opting for second-hand furniture or other practical solutions helped us avoid unnecessary debt. It allowed us to focus on building a stable financial foundation instead of trying to keep up with an ideal that wasn't realistic for our stage in life.

The Stress of Financial Pressure

Financial stress can weigh heavily on a marriage, especially for a young couple. As a man, I've seen how the pressure to provide and meet expectations can be overwhelming. It's crucial to work together as a team, communicate openly about financial goals, and keep perspective.

By avoiding credit card traps, managing expectations, and prioritizing what truly matters, we were able to navigate those early challenges. It wasn't easy, but the lessons we learned along the way have been invaluable for our financial journey and our marriage.

Final Thoughts on Money and Marriage

Conflict Resolution and Communication

One of the biggest lessons I've learned is that silence can sometimes be too loud. When it comes to finances—or any aspect of marriage—avoiding communication doesn't solve problems. If there's something on your mind, share it. Being quiet doesn't help move the conversation or the relationship forward.

When it comes to managing money in a marriage, open and honest dialogue is critical. Finances are a shared responsibility, and both partners need to feel comfortable discussing their concerns, goals, and challenges.

Networking as Currency

Another important consideration is understanding that networking can be a form of currency, even if it's not monetary. For example, attending events like Christmas parties, sorority or fraternity meetings, or work functions may seem unnecessary at first glance. But these gatherings often create connections that lead to professional and financial opportunities.

Networking isn't just about what you know—it's about who you know. And that concept can be challenging to grasp, especially across different races, cultures, or upbringings. But when both partners understand and support these activities, it can lead to significant long-term benefits for the household.

Trust and Financial Systems

Trust plays a huge role in financial harmony. If one pot of shared finances doesn't work for your relationship, consider experimenting with three pots: yours, theirs, and the family's. This approach allows for individual autonomy while maintaining a shared commitment to household responsibilities.

Over time, ask yourselves the tough questions: Is keeping separate finances a matter of trust? What is it about money that causes division? Exploring these issues can lead to better understanding and stronger teamwork.

Shared Responsibilities at Home

Finances aren't just about dollars and cents; they influence every aspect of a relationship. For example, when we had young children, my wife and I shared the responsibilities of preparing for the week. On Sunday nights, I would iron the kids' clothes for the week, and we'd split tasks like getting the kids ready in the morning or taking turns with nighttime feedings.

This type of partnership extends to finances. It's about taking the burden off each other when needed and working together to keep the household running smoothly.

The Intersection of Money, Sex, and Power
In my view, money, sex, and power are interconnected forms of currency in a relationship. How a couple handles money can affect their intimacy, their balance of power, and even their overall connection. That's why it's so important to approach finances not just as a practical matter but as a relational one.

By communicating openly, dividing responsibilities fairly, and supporting each other's goals, couples can build a foundation of trust and partnership that strengthens every aspect of their marriage.

Chapter 4
Money & Kingdom Mindset

Money & Kingdom Mindset

When you've experienced a drought or a season of lack for a long time, it becomes difficult to envision a way out of financial struggles. Life can begin to resemble the saying, "mo' money, mo' problems." As I earned more money, I started to encounter more challenges. It was overwhelming.

To make any significant change in your life, having God first is essential. Every decision should involve Him. Every step taken should be directed by His guidance. If you look back at the infographic at the beginning of this book, you will see that reliance on God is the key to moving any mountain in your life.

I must confess that I was out of alignment with God's will. During my struggles in a season of financial drought, I sought answers from my close friends and family members. I hoped they could provide the help I needed. However, I found that no one could truly assist me. It wasn't until I fully surrendered everything to the Lord and said "yes" to Him in January 2023 that my situation began to change. My world felt shaken initially, but God started to move mountains in mighty and miraculous ways.

Tithing

God began to work on me in the area of tithing. This was the turning point of my financial journey. If you do not regularly tithe, you may lack discipline in managing your money. I used to try to balance my budget in my head, but this method did not work. My mind was already crowded with meetings, appointments for my children, and daily to-do lists. It is easy to overlook tithing when life is busy.

My lack of planning affected my finances. It took courage to let God lead me in this area. I struggled because I thought, God, if I tithe, then I won't have enough money to pay my bills. I felt trapped in a cycle of fear and doubt. However, as I grew spiritually, I learned to trust God more. He gave me comfort on days when my faith was weak. My relationship with Him deepened. I began to read the Word of the Lord daily. Miracles started to happen. It was incredible to witness these changes in my life.

I started to tithe consistently out of faith. One day, my finances were extremely low, and I was aware that I only had a fixed amount of money at hand. Despite this, I decided to pay my tithe. I prayed, "Holy Spirit, this is all the money I have, but I know You will take care of us." After I paid my tithes, something wonderful happened. As I drove to pick my son up from school, I received a miraculous call. Money had been deposited in my account. I checked my balance and saw that the amount I had just paid in tithes was literally doubled in another account. Needless to say (I know I looked nuts in the car to those who were next to me), I began crying and thanking the Lord for being faithful.

We must trust and believe that God will provide for our needs. I share this story to show that His promises are real. Many preachers talk about tithing regularly.

However, I want to present a real-life miracle that illustrates God's truth in our daily lives. When we give our tithes willingly, we open the door for God to work in surprising ways.

God knows our thoughts because He is all-powerful. He sees our struggles. If we are faithful on our Christian journey, He begins to place our names and faces in the hearts of others. Those people will want to help or bless us just when we need it most. On one occasion, after I faithfully paid my tithes, I met my dad to pick up something. Out of the blue, he gave me some money that I urgently needed to feed my family. He did not know I had been praying for this help.

These moments energize my spirit. I remember listening to praise music in the car when my dad handed me that money. At that moment, I felt overwhelmed with gratitude. I exited the car filled with joy and started to dance! To onlookers, I probably appeared a bit eccentric, but I did not care. They did not understand my journey. They did not witness the trials I faced or the blessings I received. I just had to rejoice.

As I danced, I noticed a young man in the distance. He watched me for a moment, then he began dancing too. This truly made me smile. It was a beautiful reminder of how joy can connect us all, even in unexpected ways. God shows up when we least expect it and often through others.

When you choose to serve the Lord, even during tough times, look for moments of joy. It is essential to remember to smile. Serving God is not always easy. However, it brings blessings. If you want to see some structure in your finances and experience miracles, tithing is necessary. It is not optional.

Tithing is at the center of God's law. The Bible reminds us of this in Proverbs 3:9, which says, "Honor the Lord with your wealth, with the first fruits of all your crops." When you aim for mountains to move in your life, tithing is essential. This act requires commitment. If you are not consistently tithing, consider changing your mindset. Even if you tithe from a place of faith, you should implement a structured approach. Tithing is non-negotiable for believers.

In 2023, God spoke a promise to me. He said He would transform my family from a state of barrenness to one of fruitfulness. This promise holds true for all His children. However, it requires our commitment to His Word. We must honor it, trust it, and remain faithful so that God can trust us in return. He is there to guide us through the process with His grace and mercy.

Financial struggles can make many people feel isolated. I know this feeling well. Yet, when you have Jesus by your side, He walks with you every step of the way. My friend, if you desire all that God has in store for you, you must commit to being a tither. Your faithfulness in this area opens doors for His blessings.

So, how should you start with tithing? Begin by taking a small step of faith. Pray for God to help you in this area and then follow through with your actions. Trust that

He will provide for your needs and watch as blessings pour into your life. Even when it feels difficult, remember that God is faithful; He will never let you down. Tithing may seem like a simple act, but it holds the power to transform our lives in miraculous ways.

Tithing doesn't have to be a daunting task. Start by setting aside 10% of your income for tithing and see how God blesses you in return. You can also set up recurring automatic payments to make it easier to consistently tithe. And always remember, tithing is not just about giving back to God, but it's also an act of trust and obedience. Trust that He will provide for you and be obedient in faithfully giving back to Him.

Kingdom Money Mindset Model

Alright, so I need your undivided attention now. Put away all distractions. This tea is going to be good. I have a confession: I absolutely love reading my Bible. After I became saved and accepted the Lord into my heart, my life changed. I was no longer blind to the truth of Scripture. I grew up in church, but I never fully understood many passages in the Bible. Sometimes, they felt hard to read and comprehend.

Like the song "Amazing Grace" says, "Amazing grace how sweet the sound that saved a wretch like me! I once was lost, but now I'm found; was blind, but now I see." I was blind in many areas of my life because I lacked a true relationship with the Lord. God desires to bring you out of your wilderness season. He wants to move mountains for you, but you must develop a relationship with Him.

I cherish my relationship with God. As I followed Him, my situation began to improve.

Before, I didn't understand parts of the Bible. Now I know it was because I didn't have a consistent daily relationship with Him. Once God became my friend, I looked forward to reading my Bible. Each day, I sought to receive my instructions. How did I reach this point? It was simple: I said "yes" to the Lord. Wherever He led me, I followed. It felt like He removed a blindfold from my eyes, and I began to understand God more rapidly.

On days when life became hectic, I often felt frustrated. I realized then that I hadn't prayed or read my Bible. In those moments, I would say, "Holy Spirit, I need a fresh word so that I am not leaning on my own understanding." I recalled the words of Proverbs 3:5-6: "Trust in the Lord with all your heart and lean not on your own understanding; in all your ways submit to him, and he will make your paths straight."

How to Develop a Kingdom Money Mindset?

"For truly I say to you, if anyone says to this mountain, 'Be removed and cast into the sea,' and does not doubt in his heart but believes that what he says will happen, it will be done for him" (Mark 11:23). This verse highlights the incredible power of faith. When you believe deeply, you can make an impact. A mountain can represent any challenge or obstacle in your life. It can be financial difficulties, personal struggles, or spiritual battles.

Next, you should understand the power of desire. Desire

is not just wanting something. It is a strong feeling that pushes you to seek God. Whatever you desire, take it to God in prayer. Believe that He hears you.

Jesus reminds us, "Therefore I say unto you, what things soever ye desire, when ye pray, believe that ye receive them, and ye shall have them" (Mark 11:24). This means that prayer is essential. Pray with expectation. Your prayers should express your desires clearly.

To develop a Kingdom money mindset, follow this model:
1. Have faith in God
2. Desire
3. Pray
4. Believe
5. Receive

It starts with "yes!" When I said "yes" to God, I opened the door for Him to lead me. I accepted His will and His way for my life. After I made this decision, everything seemed chaotic. Yet, God was working behind the scenes. He was putting the pieces of my life together like a magnificent puzzle. Faith does not mean everything will be perfect. Your circumstances may still be challenging.

This was hard for me because I am very analytical. I like to understand everything clearly. As I prayed for God to strengthen my faith, I spent more time in His presence. I began to see my reality shift. I no longer focused on the noisy world around me. Instead, I saw how God was moving mountains and providing for His plans in my life. If we want to see change, we must take action. If we don't move, the mountain won't move. It begins with our faith. Put aside doubt and fear. Start moving forward. I learned that God cannot bless what we refuse to act upon. If He has given us an assignment, we must work diligently until it is completed.

Think of it like school. Every student has assignments with deadlines. If God has called you to start a business or create a new income stream, there is a divine purpose behind it. Understand that God places desires in our hearts for a reason. He may want us to pursue entrepreneurship, but we must remember that it is a process. God desires to ensure we have both earthly and spiritual maturity. This maturity is necessary for us to be good stewards of His blessings.

As my faith grew and I walked closely with God, I started to see His amazing works. I noticed little to no results when I sought clients or posted about my services without God's guidance. However, when I obeyed God's instructions, everything changed. These instructions often came from reading my Bible, praying, or being aware of the signs He showed me. Following His lead, I began to receive what I needed. God started to open doors and send clients my way.

This does not mean that all my financial issues were solved immediately. I understood that each client was an assignment. Every assignment came with its own lessons that were meant to prepare me for the next level that God intended for me. It is important to remember that starting small is okay. Building a strong foundation takes time.

When you unlock your faith in God, you realize He is always with you. He will never leave you. With this understanding, you possess everything you need to face your challenges. When you speak to your mountain, it will be moved. Following the model of faith, God will provide you with the strategies, power, and authority necessary to overcome obstacles.

In Mark 11:28-29, it is written, "And say unto him, by what authority doest thou these things? And who gave thee this authority to do these things? And Jesus answered and said unto them, 'I will also ask of you one question, and answer me; and I will tell you by what authority I do these things.'" This passage emphasizes the authority we have through Christ.

As you nourish your relationship with God, you begin to feel the presence of Jesus within you. He grants you the power and authority to conquer any mountain in your life. Trust in this promise. It is through faith and obedience that we rise above our challenges.

When God gave me vivid visions and the desire to start a business, I experienced these moments while riding alone in my car. In my visions, I saw joy and successful businesses. It was a beautiful sight. However, I did not see the difficult journey in between. The struggles were hard. I cried many times in the shower, saying, "God, I know what You told me to do, but this is hard. It feels like too much." I often questioned whether I was the right person for this task.

Your circumstances may also seem impossible, but

remember that Matthew 19:26 states, "With God all things are possible." My husband and I were not just financially strained; we were truly struggling. I thought, God, how can I start this business when I have no money and face so many challenges? I was a mother to three children under the age of five. I managed a full-time job across five territories in two states. At the same time, I tried to build a startup by faith after several failed attempts.

God often waits for our situation to seem completely impossible. This way, He can reveal His glory. God will send unexpected help when you feel lost. He might send someone to provide meals when you don't know how your family will eat. He might even arrange for someone to look after your children so you can work on the book He asked you to write. When you trust God and have faith, He will guide you through each step of your journey.

God tested me with various business ideas to prepare me for the one He was ready to bless at the right time. For many years, I faced rejection, failures, and betrayal. I felt like an outcast. Deep down, I knew I had many gifts. Yet, I held back because of fear. Despite these obstacles, I clearly heard God's call. He promised to take my family from a place of barrenness to one of fruitfulness. It would be done in such a way that nobody could deny it was God's hand at work.

I wrestled with fear and questioned the voice of God. However, when God anoints you and assigns you to fulfill your purpose for His Kingdom, He will send confirmation. He brings in angelic reinforcements, disciples, clergy, and prophets to affirm His Word and your mission. Realize that through carrying out God's assignment, you will find your financial deliverance. This journey is not about doing what you want. It is about fulfilling what He has called you to do.

Whenever I attempted to get in God's way and do things my own way, I faced resistance. I experienced redirection. At times, God was silent. This was His way of guiding me. However, when I chose to be obedient and followed His instructions, I witnessed miraculous results. This happened every time.

To be free from a defeated money mindset, you must release fear and doubt. Let go of the spirits of delay and procrastination. As I entered my appointed season, I could no longer allow weak faith to hold me back. I needed to pursue everything that God had for my family and me. I refused to let fear of others' opinions control my actions.

Hide Joshua 1:9 in your heart and recite it daily: "Have not I commanded thee? Be strong and of a good courage; be not afraid, neither be thou dismayed: for the Lord thy God is with thee whithersoever thou goest." While reading Joshua 1, I observed that this phrase was repeated three times. The number three in the Bible signifies divine wholeness, completeness, and perfection.

This repetition serves as a powerful reminder. It reassures us that we are never alone. God is always with us. Since God repeated this phrase three times, it is a whole, complete, and perfected Word from the

Lord concerning His children. Anything you feel that you cannot accomplish in life can be achieved through Christ. The Bible tells us this in Philippians 4:13: "I can do all things through Christ which strengtheneth me." This verse stresses an important point: You cannot reach your full potential or receive your complete deliverance if you do not go through Christ.

Your deliverance involves many aspects of life. It may relate to your marriage, finances, or other challenges. But remember, achieving true success cannot happen unless Christ leads the way. Your relationship with Christ is crucial. It is through this connection that you will gain the vital guidance you need. You must follow Him. If you try to navigate life alone, you will only get so far. You won't be able to receive all that He has planned for you.

The key component of this process, as mentioned in Mark 11:24, is prayer: "Therefore I say unto you, What things soever ye desire, when ye pray, believe that ye receive them, and ye shall have them." Prayer is your lifeline. It helps you stay linked to God. Through consistent communication with Him, you will receive the necessary instructions to overcome your financial obstacles. Without God's influence, your situation will not improve.

On days when I felt overwhelmed or too busy to pray, everything in my life seemed disorganized. Life has a way of becoming chaotic when we lose our connection with God. If you want God to bless your business, income, income streams, family, finances, or career, you need to stay connected to the vine. Jesus said, "I am the vine; you are the branches. If you remain in me and I in you, you will bear much fruit; apart from me you can do nothing" (John 15:5). This connection is vital for your success.

When we talk about "fruit," it refers to the results of our actions. Take a moment to reflect on specific desires, such as getting your student loans paid off. You might think it starts with a simple phone call to a customer service agent, but here's where prayer comes in. If you call on Jesus in prayer, He will put your name on someone's heart. That person might reach out to you with helpful information you had not even requested. In return, this will help you pay off your student loan debt so you can reallocate the money you would be spending on that toward your Kingdom assignment. (Excuse me, I digressed for a moment because that is one of my testimonies.)

The heavenly strategy I received about being relieved of my student loans was to go to the Public Service Loan Forgiveness (PSLF) page on studentaid.gov to prepare and sign a PSLF form. If you're employed by a government agency or not-for-profit organization, you might be eligible for the PSLF Program. The PSLF Program forgives the remaining balance on your Direct Loans. (Excuse me while I celebrate all over again because WON'T HE DO IT?!)

For the mountain to be moved, understand that you must stay connected to the vine—His Word—and truly believe in God with all of your heart. I mean, like really believe He is who He says He is!

God is:
- Jehovah Jireh: The Lord will provide
- Jehovah Rapha: The Lord will heal
- Jehovah Shalom: The Lord our peace
- Jehovah Nissi: The Lord our banner
- Jehovah Tsidkenu: The Lord our righteousness
- Jehovah Raah: The Lord is our shepherd
- Jehovah Shammah: The Lord is always present

I often sing the song "He's Got the Whole World In His Hands" to my children because it reminds me that God created the universe. He is in control of everything. He is the author of all things. God can use social media to bring you a divine connection that can change your life entirely. Sometimes, He sends a wind with your name across someone's desk. They may say, "I wrote her name down, and I want her to lead my team." This is just one step closer to where God wants you to be. It brings you nearer to what He desires for you.

Say "yes" to God. Have faith in Him. Believe that He will fulfill His promises. Once you surrender your financial problems, burdens, and anxiety, you must allow Him to lead. God will surprise you with how He works things out. You may not see the path clearly now. That is okay. Just follow His lead. Do the work He instructs you to do. I have seen favoritism in many settings. Some individuals get chosen because of personal preferences. It's easy to feel overlooked in such situations. But please remember, God has not forgotten you. When you walk with God, you enjoy His favor. His favor is greater than any man's approval.

I have never desired favor or accolades from people in high positions. My goal is to please God with all my efforts. God spoke to my spirit one day. He said, "Alicia, you are My beloved daughter, and you are a friend of God." To know I am a friend of God and His beloved daughter is a profound blessing. No earthly reward can compete with that. Remember, being favored by God is sustainable. His favor will come to you as a result of your obedience and faithfulness.

Alicia Fitts

EXPERT HIGHLIGHT
Bishop Mark Walden

Pastor, House of God COGIC- Thomson, GA
Author I Speaker I Leader
Website: www.bishopmarkwalden.com

Meet Bishop Mark Walden

Bishop Mark Walden is a distinguished spiritual leader and community figure based in Thomson, Georgia. With over six decades of dedicated service to the Church of God in Christ (COGIC), he has made significant contributions to both his congregation and the broader community.

Humble beginnings: born in Louisville, Georgia, Bishop Walden pursued his education in the Jefferson County School System and furthered his theological studies at the C.H. Mason Theological Seminary in Atlanta, Georgia. He embraced his faith in 1960, becoming a member of the Friendly Church of God in Christ under the leadership of Elder Cleveland Woods, Sr. Before his calling to ministry, he served in various capacities, including Chairman of the Deacon Board and Sunday School Superintendent.

In 1970, Bishop Walden accepted his calling into the ministry and was licensed in 1971. He was ordained as an Elder in 1973 and founded the House of God Church of God in Christ in Thomson, Georgia. Under his leadership, the church has grown and expanded, including the dedication of a new sanctuary in 1999 and the acquisition of a 1.5-million-dollar shopping plaza for church use. He also established the Shalom Temple Church of God in Christ in Sandersville, Georgia, in 2003.

Bishop Walden's leadership roles within the COGIC organization are extensive. He served as the Superintendent of the Augusta District and was appointed as the Prelate of the Northern Georgia Second Ecclesiastical Jurisdiction in 1994, officially inaugurated in 1995. His contributions have been recognized with several honors, including the "Most Distinguished Leader" award by the C.H. Mason Theological Seminary in 2007 and the Men Perfecting Men of Valor Award during the 111th Holy Convocation in 2018.

On a personal note, Bishop Walden was married to the late Dorothy J. Walden for over six decades, and together they raised ten children with a host of grandchildren and great-great-grandchildren. In March 2024, he married Lady CJ Walden. His life and ministry continue to inspire many within and beyond his community.

Beginnings and Calling

Question: Can you share the story of how you first felt called by God to start your mechanical company and later build your ministry?

It really started with humble beginnings. I was working at Augusta Chemical Company, and I needed some extra money. A friend told me about a shop that needed someone to clean up. I started working there on Mondays while still holding my job at the chemical company.

Eventually, I got interested in the mechanical side of things—particularly transmissions. I would clean the shop, take transmissions apart for the builders, and clean them up. Over time, by watching and paying attention, I learned how to put them back together. I never went to school for it—it was simply a gift from God. It was like solving a puzzle, and every piece had a place.

God gave me the ability to understand it. That's how I learned transmissions—by doing, by watching, and by believing that I could.

Hearing God's Call to Start a Business

Question: That's amazing! What was the moment when you realized God was calling you to start your own business?

Well, after some time, I worked my way up to being the head mechanic in the shop. I fixed everything—transmissions, cars, school buses, you name it. But I noticed something: I was doing most of the work, but I wasn't getting paid fairly.

I talked to the owner about it, but he told me he had to be "fair" to everyone else. Meanwhile, I found out he had told someone else, "The ones making the money in this shop are those two Black guys"—talking about me and another brother working there.

At that moment, God placed a thought in my spirit: "If you can make money for him, you can make money for yourself."

I started working on transmissions after hours in my own small building, using just two old tables. I was building transmissions for about four different shops. They would bring them to me, I'd fix them, and they'd come back and pick them up.

When the owner went on vacation and left me in charge, I realized even more that I was already running things—but without the reward. So when he came back, I handed him my notice. I backed up my two old trucks, took my tools home, and officially stepped out on my own—even before I had a full business license.

Question: You started without the license?

(Laughs) Yeah, I didn't even know I needed one at first. But when God's hand is on it, it's already blessed. That's Kingdom mindset.

Facing Challenges

Question: I'm trying not to cry hearing this. You clearly faced a lot—being overlooked because of race, being underpaid. Was your spouse supportive when you made the leap?

Honestly? No, not at first. I didn't tell her. When I backed the trucks up to the house with my tools and equipment, that's when she found out I had quit. (Laughs) She went into a rage!

We had kids, bills—and here I was, stepping out without warning. But I told her, "We'll live as if we gonna live." I trusted that God was going to provide.

Before I even had the building, I was building transmissions in the kitchen! After we ate dinner, I'd set up chairs and a board to make a workbench. I'd lay newspaper down and rebuild transmissions right there. I'd charge $195 for each one.

Faith, Trust, and Provision

Question: How did your trust and faith in God help you with provision and success?

God gave me the wisdom. He gave me the gift. I just had to trust Him and walk it out.

You have to have faith. You have to believe that when God says He'll do something, He is able to do it. I didn't doubt. I just kept moving forward, even when it looked impossible.

Question: That's powerful. I'm also curious—naturally, with faith, we also have to steward well. Did you and your wife budget or do practical things to manage the business?

Yes, we did. My wife, Dorothy, took care of the finances. We partnered together. She made sure the money was managed right. That's important too—faith and stewardship go hand in hand.

Advice for Those Struggling with a Defeated Money Mindset

Question: Today, you live abundantly compared to where you started. For those who are struggling with a defeated money mindset, what daily habits or thought processes helped you maintain a Kingdom mindset to unlock God's abundance?

I'm a hard believer that if God promises you something, He is able to perform it.
You can't be half-in and half-out. You have to fully trust Him and walk in faith.

But it's not just about belief—faith requires action.

Belief alone won't get you there. Faith will take you where belief can't.

That's the key. Walk by faith. Trust God. Steward well. And remember—God will never leave you nor forsake you.

Chapter 5
Planning for Life's Major Events

"'For I know the plans I have for you,' declares the Lord, 'plans to prosper you and not to harm you, plans to give you hope and a future. Then you will call on me and come and pray to me, and I will listen to you. You will seek me and find me when you seek me with all your heart.'" — Jeremiah 29:11-13

Starting a business might be an option for some people. For me, it became a necessity. In my first year of marriage, I faced my first failed attempt at starting a business. I was navigating through an unfamiliar time in my life. Everything felt new. I was a newlywed, newly pregnant, and about to have my first baby. Each change brought its own challenges. I was also working a new job in a role that I had never done before. On top of that, I was trying to start a business.

You might wonder, Why not delay the business venture? I was trying to be proactive. I wanted to get ahead of the potential financial issues my husband and I might face after our baby arrived. We were not prepared for parenthood. God blessed us with the gift of a child. Our plans took a turn, and we felt the weight of the storm approaching.

My husband and I have known each other for many years. We first met when he was just two years old. I was only one. We don't remember our first encounter. Those memories were shared with us by our parents. Let's explore how God designs divine connections.

It all began when my mom met my husband's mom. This meeting happened over the phone. My husband's mom,

Tanga, was making a sales call to my mother's workplace. During the call, she mentioned a job opportunity. My mom applied for the job and got it. From there, they became friends. This connection set the stage for my husband and me to meet each other in high school.

He proposed when I was twenty-two years old, and we got married when I turned twenty-five. Looking back, I see that we ended up in a tough financial situation. This stemmed from not discussing our individual financial situations before marriage. We didn't create a life plan together. Instead, we jumped headfirst into life without sufficient preparation.

Life could have overwhelmed us. Yet, by the grace of God, we made it through. We faced several difficult seasons because of our lack of preparation. I wouldn't want to change my story, even with the challenges. This was a major oversight for both of us. We didn't seek proper marital and financial counseling. This could have guided us in navigating our marriage more smoothly and thoughtfully.

I believe God makes no mistakes. Even when we try to control our lives, He does not hold our errors against us. It's important to remember that God is in control. I had to step out of the driver's seat of my life. In that seat, I was making many wrong decisions. I needed to let God take the wheel. Despite all my struggles, God still had a plan for me and my family. He never gave up on me. He wanted to bless me even amid my marital problems and financial troubles.

When I look back, I see the weight of my financial mistakes. My husband and I faced many difficulties together. Yet, I also see the beauty of God's grace. With each challenge, I learned valuable lessons. I wanted to surrender completely to God's will. This was not easy. It required courage and faith. God took my "yes" and transformed it into a journey of healing.

My husband and I moved through a wilderness season that felt long and arduous. Each setback was tough, but it brought growth. Through hard work and discipline, we discovered deliverance. We became equipped to help others. We shared our experiences with family members because sharing our journey brings hope to those facing similar struggles.

How I Would Have Advised Myself from the Ages of 18-25

In this age group, many are in an exciting phase of life where everything is full of possibilities. By the age of twenty-one, I entered the financial industry as a head teller. I quickly moved up the ladder with many promotions. However, I had no guidance on what to do with my increased income. Yes, I was advised to increase my retirement contributions. However, I did not consider other important financial decisions.

By twenty-five, I wish I had planned better for my future. I was engaged at the time. My now-husband and I should have talked about our goals. We never discussed how many kids we might want someday. Instead, we just lived our best married life. We made decisions as we went along.

A lack of planning can feel overwhelming. I learned this the hard way. After our experiences and mistakes, my husband and I know better now. Smart financial moves can set you up for success.

Looking back, I realize the importance of having a plan. Planning involves discussing your dreams and goals together. This means you and your spouse create a shared vision. Having these conversations helps avoid surprises later. Finances are just one piece of the puzzle that can impact your entire life. In the upcoming sections, I'll dive deeper into specific financial tips and advice that I wish I had known during this phase of life.

Things You NEED to Start Doing Right Now

Start saving ASAP - I genuinely wish someone had pounded this point into my head back when I was unsuspectingly strolling through my early 20s. Saving money may not sound thrilling at first; after all, the allure of doing something "fun" with your paycheck often wins out. But let me tell you, getting into the habit of saving early can change your life.

Even if you can stash away only a small amount each month, it's essential to start saving. When I think of my grandmother's wise words, I feel like she is right next to me. She used to say, "I don't care if you put $5 to the side. It's the consistency that counts." Just think about it: $5 a week adds up. That's about $260 a year! Imagine what you could do with that money. You could use it for emergencies, save it for a future down payment on a house, or stow it away for retirement.

Creating and evaluating your budget is key. It's where the magic happens! Look for areas where you can cut back. For me, I bought a luxury car before I was ready. It started out as a symbol of pride but morphed into a financial burden. The moment my warranty expired, everything hit the fan. Between having kids in private daycare and unforeseen car troubles, my husband and I were scrambling. We had to start from square one with our emergency funds.

Now, here's a quick tip: You might want to consider opening a separate savings account. Visualizing your savings as distinct from your everyday spending can bolster your motivation. When you see that number slowly climbing on its own, you'll feel a sense of security. Having a safety net can do wonders for your peace of mind. You won't feel like you're walking on a financial tightrope. Instead, you'll feel ready to tackle whatever life throws your way.

Let's take a moment to look ahead. The sooner you start saving, the earlier you can confidently navigate life's major financial events. Whether it's buying a house, having children, or even preparing for retirement, savings provide the foundation you need. The goal is to build that security steadily. This feels almost like training for a marathon. It's not about how fast you can run today, but about the consistent effort over time that prepares you for the big race ahead.

Create financial goals together - If you're engaged or married, it's important to align your financial goals with your future spouse/spouse. Sit down and have an open conversation about your dreams and aspirations. Whether it's buying a home, traveling the world, or starting a family, having shared goals will help you work together toward a brighter financial future.

You want to create SMART financial goals.
　Specific
　Measurable
　Attainable
　Realistic
　Time-bound

Let's break it down with examples.

A Good SMART Financial Goal
"I will save $5,000 by the end of the year for a down payment on a house. I will achieve this by setting aside $417 each month from my paycheck into a dedicated savings account." This goal is specific, measurable, achievable, relevant, and time-bound.

- **Specific** - The goal specifies the exact amount to be saved ($5,000).
- **Measurable** - Progress toward the goal can be easily measured by tracking the monthly savings contributions.
- **Achievable** - Saving $417 per month is within the individual's budget and achievable based on their current income and expenses.
- **Relevant** - Saving for a down payment on a house

aligns with the individual's long-term financial goals.
- **Time-bound** - The goal has a specific deadline (end of the year) to provide a sense of urgency and motivation.

Let's take a look at a . . .
A Bad Financial Goal
"I want to be rich."

This goal lacks specificity, measurability, and a clear action plan. What does "rich" mean exactly? How will the person measure progress toward this goal? What steps will they take to achieve it? Without specific targets and a plan of action, it's difficult to determine whether this goal is achievable or relevant to the individual's financial situation. Remember, SMART goals provide clarity and focus, making it easier to track progress and stay motivated along the way.

You also want to prepare for setbacks. Don't get discouraged if you are unable to meet the requirements for your goal. It's most important to get back on track. You also want to keep God at the head of all your plans. Don't forget to pray and get your instructions from Christ. He will direct your path and help you achieve your plans successfully. Let God bless and be the author and finisher of your plans. Trust me, it's better His way . . .every time.

"Trust in the LORD with all thine heart; and lean not unto thine own understanding. In all thy ways acknowledge him, and he shall direct thy paths" (Proverbs 3:5-6).

Invest in yourself - Your education, skill development, and career are some of the most valuable assets you have. Whether it's pursuing higher education, learning new skills, or advancing in your current job, invest in yourself. The more you grow professionally, the greater your earning potential and financial stability will become. I attract elevation and promotion because I am constantly taking things to the next level. It's easy to get distracted and look at what your neighbor is doing, but you need to keep your focus on God and the lane (or lanes) He's placed you in.

Invest in your PUSH circle. You are a product of your environment. Jesus's disciples were a diverse group of individuals from various backgrounds and professions. They were former fishermen, tax collectors, zealots, etc. The disciples helped Jesus in a plethora of ways. They offered Jesus companionship and support, assisted him in teaching and preaching, witnessed miracles, provided practical support, and did missionary work.

The people in your circle need to be supportive of your goals and plans in life; they need to encourage and uplift you to be the best version of yourself. My PUSH circle recognizes gifts on the inside of me that I may not be cognizant of or utilizing; they push me to work at my greatest potential. As you invest in yourself, you need to invest in attracting solid friendships, prayer partners, and business relationships that can help you grow and flourish.

Here's what to look for when establishing your PUSH circle.

- **P** - Positive influencers - Surround yourself with people who bring positivity into your life and uplift you.
- **U** - Unwavering support - Ask God to send you individuals who offer unwavering support and encouragement in your endeavors.
- **S** - Shared goals - Connect with people who share similar goals and aspirations, allowing you to push each other toward success.
- **H** - Helpful feedback - Embrace individuals who provide constructive criticism and feedback to help you grow and improve. We can all use mentorship to blossom into our full potential.
- **Circle** - Community of growth - Cultivate a close-knit community of individuals committed to mutual growth and development.

So, your PUSH circle consists of positive influencers, unwavering support, shared goals, helpful feedback, and a community of growth. These are the people who help you elevate to become a better person.

Protect your loved ones - Now, I know it's not the most pleasant topic, but it's crucial to think about insurance and taking care of yourself. Life, health, and disability insurance might not seem important now, but they provide a safety net for you and your family in case the unexpected happens. Because I had several unexpected pregnancies, I needed reliable short-term disability insurance after I was out of work for 6-8 weeks.

If you are employed, you need a personal policy in addition to the short-term policy offered by your employer. I had a cesarean section (C-section), which required me to not work for six weeks to heal properly. I have some experience as a former employee benefits specialist and remember helping individuals select proper healthcare. When making life plans, you certainly want to take into consideration the cost of healthcare for a family and analyze what your budget can handle.

After the age of twenty-six, healthcare is mandatory. As I matured, I began to understand the importance of taking care of my health and always striving to eat healthier. Even though fast food is a quick go-to option, it's not the best solution. If we don't eat healthy foods and take care of our bodies, we can't work or run our businesses. Your health decisions and choices affect your financial sustainability.

Also, please do not neglect the power of nourishing your mind and remembering to unplug. If you want to live to protect your loved ones, you have to first take care of yourself. When you are on a mission to be the best version of yourself, the enemy will try to attack your mind and/or health. That is because he is on a mission to do anything he can to block you from God's blessings. You must remove yourself from distractions and spend at least thirty minutes a day praying, reading your Bible, and talking to God about your life. Thank Him for being your friend and guide throughout life.

Life Insurance
Life insurance might not be the most thrilling topic to dive into, but let me tell you, it's crucial—especially if you're in your early twenties and navigating the wild terrain

of adulthood. Think of it this way: We don't splurge on expensive handbags we can't afford. Instead, we invest in life insurance policies to protect our future. So, here are some straightforward tips to help you navigate this important aspect of planning for life's major events.

Know Your Needs
You might not have a family or a mortgage yet, but don't let that fool you into thinking life insurance isn't relevant. Consider any debts you carry—having student loans or credit card debt means you have responsibilities. If something happened to you, would your loved ones be left with a mountain of financial burdens? That's the last thing you want.

Start Early
Retirement may seem like it's eons away, but the sooner you secure life insurance, the better. The younger and healthier you are, the more affordable your policy will be. Locking in a low rate now means you're protected, even if life's unpredictable twists come your way. My mentor, Dr. Nikkie Pryce, always encourages me to get M.A.D. (make a decision) now. Don't wait until coverage becomes a stretch for your budget.

Keep It Simple
Embrace term life insurance; it is your straightforward ally. Unlike other policies, it's easier to understand and tends to be budget friendly. Plus, you can select a term that aligns with your life—ten, twenty, or even thirty years. It really is as simple as that!

Avoid Overkill
Here, I want you to remember that having enough coverage is essential, but going overboard isn't wise. Assess your financial responsibilities. Only pay for the coverage that truly meets your needs.

Check Out Workplace Options
Sometimes, your job might offer life insurance bundled in as part of your benefits. While it's a nice perk, don't fall into the trap of believing it's enough on its own. Best practice? Supplement it with your own policy if needed.

Think About The Future
Life throws curveballs, especially when you're young. Remember what the Bible says, "Do not boast about tomorrow, for you do not know what a day may bring" (Proverbs 27:1). You're likely to hit major milestones like marriage, homeownership, or parenthood. Be proactive—review your insurance coverage regularly and adjust as life changes.

Shop Around
You wouldn't settle for the first car that caught your eye, would you? Why do so with an insurance policy? Prices and coverage can vary significantly across providers, so invest time comparing quotes and finding what best suits you.

Keep It Real
If navigating this feels overwhelming, don't hesitate to ask for help. Seek guidance from a financial advisor (like yours truly) or an insurance agent. They can break things down into language that makes sense. And always

ensure you can budget for the policy amount.

Now, I get it. Life insurance isn't the most glamorous or exciting topic, but treating it with the importance it deserves is all about caring for yourself and your loved ones while planning for your future. It's a practical, loving act. After all, the stronger your financial foundation, the better you can provide for those who matter most. Ultimately, think of life insurance as a vital part of your long-term strategy. It may not be the flashiest part of financial planning, but it is worth every bit of consideration. Your peace of mind and ability to support family in times of need depend on it.

Live Within Your Means - We've all felt the pressure of scrolling through social media and thinking everyone is living their best lives. They're splurging on the latest gadgets or rocking designer clothes. It's easy to feel inadequate and think you need to keep up. But let me tell you, living beyond your means is a slippery slope. Believe me, I've been there. I once found myself in a financial mess because I wanted to project an image of success. I thought, I deserve this! But do you know what I truly deserved? The peace of mind that comes with not worrying about how my next bill would get paid.

Living within your means isn't about deprivation. It's about making choices that align with your values. Focus on what really matters to you. You might find joy in experiences like going on family vacations or spending quality time with friends. These moments create memories that last far longer than any flashy item. Imagine spending that money on a weekend away with loved ones instead of a designer handbag. Doesn't that sound better?

As millennials, we often face the challenge of balancing societal expectations with our personal finances. Consider my experience with the luxury car I bought. Sure, it was shiny and new. It took my breath away in the showroom, but I failed to see the bigger picture. The payments on that vehicle drained thousands from my budget. I could have redirected that money to creating memories or building my future. Let me remind you, there is no such thing as "lost time." It's never too late to make better choices.

Another key point to remember is that it's not about how much money you make; it's about how you manage it. A high salary doesn't guarantee financial security. Many high earners live paycheck to paycheck while those who earn modestly are building wealth. So, instead of obsessing over what others have, focus on crafting a budget that reflects your situation and goals. When writing out your budget, consider fixed costs like rent and variable expenses like groceries. Being diligent about these details is vital.

The Bible teaches us a lot about stewardship. Proverbs 27:1 says, "Do not boast about tomorrow, for you do not know what a day may bring." This verse is a great reminder of the unpredictability of life. You may find yourself facing unexpected obstacles, so having your finances in order can make all the difference. Prepare for the unforeseen.

When you embrace living within your means, you take a powerful step toward financial freedom. This mindset allows for growth. It creates room in your life for opportunities and dreams. It encourages intentional spending and mindful living. Try asking yourself, "Will this purchase align with my goals?" If the answer is no, let it go.

Plan for Parenthood - I know, the excitement can make it tough to focus on practicality. Children are amazing little beings that bring immeasurable joy. But let's be real: Kids can also be incredibly expensive. From the moment they arrive, costs start piling up. Think of everything—diapers, daycare, doctor visits, and don't forget about school supplies and extracurricular activities! The list seems endless, doesn't it?

By planning, you're not just preparing for the expenses. You're also giving yourself freedom and peace of mind. Imagine this: You're pregnant and instead of stressing about finances, you're able to enjoy craving that pickles-and-ice-cream combo. This kind of preparation allows you to put thought into budgeting for future needs that come with parenthood. You can create savings accounts specifically for those early years or future educational needs. Trust me, considering education costs early on can prevent future headaches.

Now, let's dive a bit deeper into budgeting. Start with estimating your current expenses and add in the anticipated costs of having children. Use simple calculations to understand your financial landscape. You might think about it this way: If your rent is $X and your groceries are $Y, then adding another "little human" whose needs require $Z monthly will give you a clearer picture. You can also consider possible external assistance from family or government support for childcare.

Don't worry about getting everything perfect in your planning. It's a journey of learning and growth. Just like parenthood, you won't have all the answers from day one. Instead, approach this with an open heart and mind. You will refine your plan as your needs evolve and your family grows. The beauty of this experience is you get to learn together with your child.

Don't Forget about Retirement - As we wrap up the topic of planning for parenthood, let's shift our focus to a theme that can feel distant yet is just as vital: retirement. You might think it's a realm meant for your parents or grandparents. Let me assure you, the earlier you start thinking about retirement, the better off you'll be. It's often said that time is money, and when it comes to retirement, this couldn't be truer! Compound interest works in your favor when you give it more time to grow. So why wait?

Think about this: When you're nearing the end of your career, wouldn't it be great to glance into your bank account and smile instead of freeze in fear? Starting to save now can transform that potential panic into peace. Consider taking advantage of employer-sponsored retirement plans like a 401(k). With these plans, your employer may even match your contributions up to a certain percentage. That's essentially free money! If your workplace doesn't offer a 401(k), don't fret. You can still set up an individual retirement account (IRA) and start building your nest egg independently.

Now, I know the numbers can seem overwhelming. Let's break it down. Picture this: If you save just $200 a month starting at age twenty-five and average a 7% annual return, you could potentially amass close to $1 million by the time you retire at sixty-five. Yes, $1 million! Doesn't that sound good? But if you wait until you're thirty-five, you would need to save about $400 each month to reach that same goal. It really shows how starting early pays off in the long run.

Just like the Scripture reminds us, "Do not boast about tomorrow, for you do not know what a day may bring" (Proverbs 27:1). This isn't just about finances; it's about taking action today for what's to come tomorrow. Life is uncertain, which is why having a plan feels comforting. What's more, contributing to your retirement isn't just an obligation. It's a commitment to your future self. It's a way to ensure you can enjoy life when the daily grind ends.

As someone who has danced through financial ups and downs, I can share that setting aside money for retirement felt like a burden at first. But as I began to grasp the larger picture, it turned into empowerment. I felt proud knowing I was securing not just my future but that of my loved ones as well. And you know what? It changed my mindset completely. I went from feeling defeated about my financial situation to actively working on it with a mindset grounded in faith.

Now, let's get practical. Take a few minutes each month to review and adjust your retirement contributions as your income changes. If you get a raise, think about allocating a percentage of that increase to your retirement savings. It's this steady and mindful approach that will lead to financial freedom when the time comes to enjoy life's rewards—and you won't have to rely on anyone else.

Don't let retirement be an afterthought. Remember that this journey is yours. Accept it as a part of the financial narrative you're writing. By taking these steps, you're not only putting money aside for the future but also demonstrating that you value your financial stability.

As you step into this new chapter of life, keep your eye on the bigger picture. Remember, it's your journey, and with Christ by your side, you can conquer any financial mountain. Trust that you're on the right path and seek guidance when needed. Just as Philippians 4:13 states, "I can do all things through Christ who strengthens me." Let that verse resonate with you as you build your financial foundation. You've got the tools. Now go out and shape your future!

EXPERT HIGHLIGHT
Sherri Chance & Vondesa Lee

Authors I Realtors I Entrepreneurs
Website: www.nextmove.realestate/agents/1773168/Vondesa%2BLee
Website: www.nextmove.realestate/agents/1773194/Sherri%2BChance
Facebook: Vondesa Lee, Next Move Real Estate
Facebook: Sherri Chance Realtor

Meet Sherri Chance

Sherri Chance is a seasoned real estate professional based in Rincon, Georgia, affiliated with Next Move Real Estate. With over 23 years of experience in sales and marketing, she has honed her skills in fostering strong client relationships and delivering exceptional service. Her extensive background includes buying, selling, and managing properties, as well as flipping homes, which has provided her with a comprehensive understanding of the real estate market.

Sherri obtained her real estate license through the Augusta School of Real Estate and has since become a member of the Statesboro Board of Realtors, the National Association of Realtors, and the Georgia Multi-Listing System. She collaborates closely with her business partner, Vondesa Lee, under the brand "Your GA Property Duo," assisting clients in communities such as Rincon, Statesboro, Brooklet, Portal, and Millen.

Known for her cheerful and relaxed demeanor, Sherri strives to make the home-buying and selling process as smooth and enjoyable as possible for her clients. In her personal life, she enjoys spending time with her family, including her grandson Bennett, and engaging in activities like cooking, entertaining, fishing, swimming, and boating with her dog, Tuck.

Meet Vondesa Lee

Vondesa Lee is a dedicated real estate professional and co-founder of Your GA Property Duo, based in Rincon, Georgia.

With a passion for helping individuals and families achieve their real estate goals, Vondesa has built a solid reputation for providing personalized, high-quality service in buying, selling, and investing in real estate.

Her expertise extends beyond traditional sales, as she works diligently to understand her clients' needs, offering valuable insight into property management and investment opportunities. Vondesa is committed to ensuring her clients have a seamless and stress-free experience, whether they are first-time home buyers or seasoned investors.

As a proud member of the Statesboro Board of Realtors, National Association of Realtors, and Georgia Multi-Listing Service, Vondesa continues to expand her knowledge of the ever-evolving real estate market. Together with her business partner, Sherri Chance, Vondesa specializes in serving the communities of Rincon, Statesboro, Brooklet, Portal, and Millen, delivering results that exceed expectations.

Outside of her professional life, Vondesa is deeply rooted in family, valuing time spent with loved ones and enjoying outdoor activities. She is committed to continuous personal growth and staying informed about the latest trends in real estate to better serve her clients.

Planning for Life's Major Events Home Buying

In this chapter, we dive into the wisdom of real estate professionals Sherri Chance and Vondesa Lee. Both bring years of experience and insight into the process of making smart financial decisions, particularly when it comes to home buying. Their advice not only helps people navigate the real estate market but also aligns with the principles of sound financial planning.

Question: When it comes to mindset and making smart decisions in the real estate market, what's one piece of financial wisdom you wish every home buyer knew?

Sherri:
Every home buyer should know the importance of setting a budget and understanding what they can truly afford. A lot of buyers get caught up thinking their starter home should be their dream home. We always emphasize that your first house might not be your forever home.

Vondesa:
Absolutely, sticking to a budget is key. When you're buying a home, there are a lot of unexpected costs that pop up, so you can't overcommit to the monthly mortgage payment. You also need to pay attention to credit card debt, as it can negatively affect your credit score and, in turn, your mortgage approval.

Sherri:
Yes, and it's essential to know that the credit score you see on platforms like Credit Karma may not be the same score your mortgage lender will use. Mortgage lenders have

their own ways of calculating it, so keep that in mind when preparing for the home-buying process. And while you're in the process, try not to go on a spending spree — even new furniture can impact your approval if it affects your credit.

Question: How should buyers determine how much house they can afford?

Sherri:
The first step is to get pre-approved for a mortgage. We don't take anyone to see homes until we know they have buying power. Local lenders are a great choice because they know the market, and they can help with appraisals and pull comps from the area to make sure the home appraises correctly.

Vondesa:
Right, and we always remind buyers that the perfect home might not exist, but the right home does. It's important to prioritize what you really need versus what you want, and be willing to compromise. No one is going to find the HGTV home on their first try.

Sherri:
And as a realtor, our job isn't just about opening doors. We provide valuable guidance throughout the entire process. We're here to help with negotiating, inspections, and even any bumps in the road during the closing process. We work closely with our clients and lenders to make sure everything runs smoothly.

Vondesa:
Also, the 28/36 rule can be a helpful guideline. This rule says

you shouldn't spend more than 28% of your gross monthly income on housing-related expenses and no more than 36% on total debts, including your mortgage, credit cards, and other loans. This rule of thumb can really help you get an idea of what's financially feasible.

Question: Does it help to have this conversation early on?

Sherri:
Definitely. We stress the importance of using local lenders because they understand the market and can sit down with buyers if needed. We've had great success with them, whereas online lenders don't always offer the same level of service.

Vondesa:
Yes, the local connection is key, and it makes a huge difference in the success of the transaction.

Question: Can you speak more on the importance of "dating" the house and not the mortgage rate?

Sherri:
The interest rate will change over time, and mortgage rates fluctuate. But the house is yours to keep. We always remind buyers not to get too caught up in the rates. If you're renting, you're paying 100% interest anyway, so focus on finding a home you can afford, and don't stress too much about the fluctuating rates. Mortgage lenders will often work with you to refinance down the line if necessary.

Question: Now, what made both of you choose a career in real estate?

Sherri:
Real estate is actually our second career. We've always been interested in homes and properties, and we wanted to pursue something we were passionate about. The opportunity to help people make their dreams come true through homeownership has been incredibly rewarding.

Vondesa:
We love working together, and we really enjoy being part of people's journey. Whether it's finding their first home or helping them upgrade, it's amazing to be a part of such a life-changing event.

Sherri:
Yes, it's been a great partnership. We've been able to build our own business while also helping others achieve their dreams.

Question: And do you have plans to expand your team or grow your business in the future?

Sherri:
At this stage in our careers, our goal is to help others succeed. We don't want the added responsibility of becoming brokers with all the extra demands. We're able to help our clients without that extra layer, and we're focusing on making a difference in their lives.

Vondesa:
It's all about creating the best possible experience for our clients, without getting bogged down by all the administrative tasks. We have a great level of support from our broker, and that's key to our flexibility.

Question: Do you have any closing remarks?

Sherri:
It's truly been a blessing working with each other and seeing how God has guided our journey. We're excited to continue helping people make their dreams come true.

Thank You for the Mountain

CHAPTER 6

*E*NTREPRENEURSHIP *&*
*S*TREAMS OF *I*NCOME

I have attempted entrepreneurship many times over the past eleven years. My journey began with my love for graphic design. I have a strong passion for creating visuals. This passion started over seventeen years ago. When I reflect on how my style has grown, I feel both astonished and thankful. The process has shaped me, and I believe God guided me through each step.

As you explore various entrepreneurial paths, remember that failure is part of the journey. You will experience setbacks. This is normal and should not deter you. The way you view these failures is crucial. View each failure as a learning opportunity. Just like mastering a new role at work, entrepreneurship is a process. Be appreciative of your failures and successes because each experience teaches you valuable lessons.

Consider this wisdom from the Bible: "And we know that in all things God works for the good of those who love him, who have been called according to his purpose" (Romans 8:28). Embrace this truth.

During my journey in entrepreneurship, I encountered a divine connection. This person graciously advised me to embrace failure instead of feeling embarrassed. Failing in some areas of my business or finances is a part of the process. It is essential to be thankful for the lessons these failures provide.

Deciding to start a business comes with hardships. These experiences inspired the title of this book, Thank You for the Mountain. Accepting Jesus as our Lord and Savior does not mean we will avoid adversity. When I reflect on how Christ suffered for us on the cross, I am reminded of His trials. He was perfect, holy, and righteous. I am flawed and imperfect. So, it is crucial to understand that I cannot expect to be excused from challenges and hardship.

If you want to pursue entrepreneurship, be prepared for disappointments. You might think you will receive a "yes," only to hear a "no." Support from family and friends may not always come when you expect it. You may have many long nights of hard work without an immediate return on your investment. There might be times when you feel foggy or uncertain about your path. It is okay to cry and let out your frustrations.

But there is always hope.

I have tried various paths in entrepreneurship, including network marketing, freelancing, photography, and even starting my own registered business. I do not see these opportunities as failures. I believe that God will make it all make sense one day.

He sees your hard work. He honors your efforts. The Bible says, "All hard work brings a profit, but mere talk leads only to poverty" (Proverbs 14:23). This verse highlights the importance of taking action and being diligent in our pursuits.

Sometimes, you might feel as though you are working without direction. You may wonder if God is listening to your prayers. Let me reassure you that He is listening. Even as a lukewarm Christian, I prayed on every birthday for ten years. My prayers were for guidance and clarity. Eleven years later, when I fully surrendered to God, He revealed an incredible truth. He promised to take my family from barrenness to fruitfulness. Even when I was a lukewarm Christian, God heard my prayers. I had moments of uncertainty, but He remained faithful. Every step you take is significant. Each experience contributes to your growth. Embrace the journey of entrepreneurship with an open heart. Your hard work will yield results. You may not see them immediately, but they are coming. Keep going.

God loves us. When I intentionally focused on building my relationship with the Lord, I found joy and happiness even during tough times. I felt secure in His love, which gave me the confidence to take action. I was able to pick up where I left off and continue working on my business. Once I resumed my work, God provided clear instructions, helpful strategies, valuable leads, and the right mentors. However, I had to seek His help to achieve true success. Psalm 121:1-2 says, "I lift up my eyes to the hills—where does my help come from? My help comes from the LORD, the Maker of heaven and earth." Remember, your help comes from the Lord.

The entrepreneurial journey can feel lonely at times. It is important to know that God is with you through every part of the process. Stay connected to Him through prayer and daily Bible reading. This connection is the blueprint for building a relationship with Christ. It leads to deeper understanding and guidance.

I have a career in business development and oversee five

territories. In the beginning, I was unsure of what I was truly getting into. The partners did not know who I was, but I kept showing up. I focused on helping people and putting in the work. Over time, God began to bless and favor me as I built professional relationships. The more you invest in your relationship with Christ, the more He will bless you. He delights in being an active presence in your life and your business journey.

Let's Talk about Starting a Business!

1. Discover Your Passion

You've found your footing in the world of entrepreneurship, but the key now is to discover your passion. Just as David was passionate about playing the harp (1 Samuel 16:23), you too must find what truly ignites your soul. This isn't just about finding a hobby; it's about unearthing something that lights a fire in you. Passion is your fuel. Without it, you'll find yourself running on empty, struggling to stay engaged.

Consider this: When you love what you do, it becomes more than just work. It transforms into a manifestation of your purpose. Remember, your journey isn't a straight shot; it's filled with twists and turns. And trust me, if you don't have that "why" tied to your passion, those long nights and hard days can feel unbearable. My first "why" was clear: I wanted to develop multiple streams of income.

Inspired by Deuteronomy 8:1-10, I envisioned a good land filled with abundance, where I wouldn't lack anything. The Bible states, "For the Lord your God is bringing you into a good land—a land with brooks, streams, and deep springs gushing out into the valleys and hills; a land with wheat and barley, vines and fig trees, pomegranates, olive oil and honey; a land where bread will not be scarce and you will lack nothing; a land where the rocks are iron and you can dig copper out of the hills." This promise resonated with me and fueled my ambition.

Let's break this down. Ask yourself a couple of key questions. What excites you? What makes you lose track of time? These can be sources of insights that reveal your passions. Perhaps you enjoyed planning gatherings, creating videos, or simply helping people solve their problems. Whatever it is, lean into it. Don't dismiss it as unimportant.

The entrepreneurial journey is often filled with harsh realities. You might experience setbacks that challenge your enthusiasm. This is part of the process. The key is to adapt and persist. Reflecting on my own experiences, I often encountered rejection and uncertainty. But remember, each "no" brings you closer to the right "yes." Each failed attempt only sharpens your understanding of what you truly want. Your passion can evolve, and that's perfectly okay.

2. Embrace Creativity
Creativity is not just an add-on; it's foundational. Genesis 1:27 says, "So God created mankind in his own image, in the image of God he created them; male and female he created them." That's right—if God, the ultimate Creator, infused creativity into us, we should embrace it! When you dive into the realm of entrepreneurship,

creativity becomes your secret weapon. It's the spark that can ignite a fire.

Think about it: Every successful venture often starts from a simple idea. Your creativity can transform that idea into something extraordinary. Picture this: You enjoy crafting unique products. Instead of just selling them at local fairs, why not expand? Use social media platforms to showcase your creative process. Take your followers behind the scenes with engaging videos or fun stories. This not only builds your brand, but it also creates personal connections with potential customers. When you think outside the box, opportunities appear where you least expect them.

Now, let's be candid. Embracing creativity means venturing into the unknown. It's about failing forward. I remember my early days with freelancing. There were times when my projects flopped miserably. But oh, did I learn! Each setback taught me something vital. I discovered I could pivot quickly. This ability to adapt is a hallmark of entrepreneurship. Instead of sulking, I shifted my focus. I repurposed ideas. I blended concepts. Success followed. Remember, creativity flourishes in environments where experimentation is encouraged.

And let's not ignore the fact that creativity often stems from necessity. During the pandemic, many people began exploring creative ways to generate income. A friend of mine started selling homemade candles online. Now, she runs a successful small business. This wasn't a result of a mapped-out plan. It stemmed from her love for creating. She found joy and purpose. She solved a problem while celebrating her creativity. What's your "candle moment"? What can you create that aligns with your passions and serves the needs of others?

3. It's OK to Start Small but Dream Big
As we shift from the engaging landscape of creativity, let's tackle another essential lesson on your entrepreneurial journey: It's okay to start small but dream big. In Matthew 13:31-32, Jesus shared a powerful parable about the mustard seed when he said, "The Kingdom of Heaven is like a mustard seed, which a man took and planted in his field. Though it is the smallest of all seeds, yet when it grows, it is the largest of garden plants and becomes a tree, so that the birds come and perch in its branches." Isn't that beautiful? It reveals a profound truth about beginnings.

Starting small doesn't minimize your ambitions. Instead, it lays a strong foundation. Think about it. The tech giant, Amazon, started in Jeff Bezos's garage as a platform to sell books. Today, it's a global empire. You see, every big enterprise once had humble beginnings. That's the beauty of entrepreneurship. It's about crafting your path, step by step. Every effort counts and each penny you save matters on the road to financial freedom. Don't underestimate the power of small actions because they accumulate over time, building momentum.

Now, getting involved in the world of finance can feel daunting when faced with societal pressures. You may look around and see friends landing great jobs or making big bucks. Your initial steps might feel insignificant. You may think, Will anyone even notice my efforts? But remember this: Those giant dreams often sprout from tiny seeds of action. It's your journey, not someone else's. Consider this approach: Create a list of three simple actions you can take this week to move toward your goal. Write down those actions even if they seem trivial. Maybe it's researching a side hustle. Maybe it's seeking advice from someone who's been there. Maybe it's crafting a budget you can share with someone for accountability. Whatever it is, make a commitment and act.

What I found transformative was when I began speaking to my "mountain of adversities." I echoed the same words God used in Genesis when He spoke light into existence. You can do the same. Speak your intentions into the universe. Declare your dreams. When I faced daunting bills, I didn't sulk. I said, "This is a season. I am capable of changing my circumstances." And guess what? Every day brought new opportunities for action.

4. Diversify Your Income

Ecclesiastes 11:2 wisely advises, "Invest in seven ventures, yes, in eight; you do not know what disaster may come upon the land." This is not just charming wisdom. It's a clarion call for stability. Relying solely on one source of income can be like flirting with danger. We need a safety net. For instance, think about what would happen if your employer suddenly shut down operations. With multiple streams of income at play, you can weather financial storms with more ease.

Consulting Services - Offering consulting services has been a game changer for me. When I started, I leveraged my knowledge of marketing and branding. With a bit of elbow grease, I landed clients who were eager for guidance. Let's be real: Every entrepreneur out there has a unique story and many experiences to share. Use that to your advantage. You can provide one-on-one consulting tailored to businesses and individuals, but don't just sell your service. Share your journey—the lessons learned and the wins (big and small). Create a personal connection. People are drawn to authenticity.

Think about your expertise. What knowledge do you have that others might find valuable? If you're good at navigating financial hurdles, why not charge for your insights? This can be a lucrative revenue stream. Plus, it allows you to build a personal brand while helping others avoid pitfalls you've encountered. When you elevate others, you elevate yourself too!

Training Workshops and Seminars - You know what else gets those wheels turning? Hosting workshops! Imagine standing in the front of a room filled with eager faces. You share what you've learned, piecing together lessons with real-world experience. It's that moment when you can tangibly see the impact of your work. You don't have to be a seasoned pro. Just share your knowledge in relatable, digestible formats.

Develop training sessions on topics such as creating a budget that actually works or navigating financial challenges with faith. People seek guidance, and you don't need to stand on a stage in a suit to give it. Make it casual yet impactful. Embrace your quirky side! The enthusiasm you bring can ignite a spark in someone else's journey. Hosting workshops also opens doors for networking and partnerships, expanding your reach further than you may have imagined.

Online Courses and E-Books - This format lets you dive deeper into specific subjects. Think about creating a series of short video lessons or writing an e-book that addresses common financial challenges. I mean, let's face it, we all learn in different ways. Some people prefer to read while others resonate with visual presentations.

Creating an online course doesn't require a huge budget or fancy software. Use what you have. Platforms like Teachable™ or Thinkific™ make things a breeze. Share your unique story alongside actionable advice. If you've conquered debt or built your savings, package that wisdom into modules or chapters. Your experiences give you credibility and can empower others to follow suit.

Membership Programs - Here's another interesting idea: launch a membership program! This could offer exclusive content, resources, and support. People love feeling like they are part of a community. Provide access to webinars, Q&A sessions, or forums where members can share their own experiences and challenges.

You can offer various membership tiers with distinct perks. Tailor packages based on what you know your audience needs. By creating an enticing value proposition, you'll attract subscribers eager to learn and grow. Plus, a steady revenue model helps ease financial stress. Consistent income from membership packages means you can invest more time in your passion projects or take a well-deserved break.

Affiliate Marketing - Don't sleep on affiliate marketing! This could be a great way to earn income by promoting products you're already using and love. Partner with companies relevant to your audience. Share authentic reviews and recommendations through your blog or on social media. Just provide your audience with helpful insight. When someone purchases through your link, you get a commission. It's as simple as that!

Choose products that align with your values and mission. You want to maintain trust with your audience. If they believe in your recommendations, that trust keeps them coming back for more. It's not just about the dollars; it's about relationship-building. And over time, this can become a sustainable revenue stream that works while you sleep.

Speaking Engagements - Let's not forget speaking engagements! Share your wealth of knowledge at conferences, industry events, and community gatherings. This positions you as an expert and creates visibility for your brand. You get to tell your story, share your experiences, and inspire those in the audience. It's about more than just making a living; it's about making an impact!

Start locally if you're nervous. Pitch to small groups or non-profits in your area. Give talks in schools or at community centers. Build your confidence and hone your presentation style. With every talk, your reputation will grow. Soon, you'll be fielding calls from event coordinators eager to have you on their stages.

Strategic Partnerships and Joint Ventures - Finally, collaborating with complementary businesses through strategic partnerships can amplify your reach. Think about partnering up with a graphic designer, a financial advisor, or even a wellness coach. Joint ventures are about synergy. By combining mutual strengths, you can offer bundles of services that your clients will find irresistible!

These collaborations create opportunities for cross-promotion. It's a means of reaching new audiences without the hefty advertising costs. Plus, the relationship-building aspect can lead to ongoing opportunities down the line. You're not alone on this journey; we're in this together.

So, take this advice to heart. In the journey toward financial freedom, diversification is your ally. Explore the possibilities. Your unique story and experiences can plant the seeds for multiple revenue streams.

5. Learn from Failure
Failure is not the end. Instead, it is a stepping stone to success. Proverbs 24:16 tells us, "For though the righteous fall seven times, they rise again." This scripture wraps itself around my heart like a warm blanket when I face setbacks. I want you to embrace this mindset. Every stumble and every fumble can teach us something valuable. Trust me, I've been there. On my journey toward financial independence, I've tripped and fallen flat on my face more times than I can count. Yet each time, I learned and grew. Remember, it is not the fall that defines you. It's how you get back up.

Embrace Setbacks as Lessons - It's easier said than done, but the more we shift our mindsets, the better we'll perform in our entrepreneurial endeavors. Think about resilience for a moment. Studies show that resilience plays a pivotal role in navigating challenges. Individuals with a resilient mindset are more likely to bounce back from disappointments. It's like building muscle. The more you flex the muscle, the stronger it becomes.

Now, let's dive a bit deeper into the psychology of failure. Research indicates that our brains are wired to recognize and learn from mistakes. Each time we fail and analyze why it happened, we create neural pathways that help us manage future challenges more effectively. For instance, let's say you tried to launch a new product or service that flopped. Instead of seeing it as a failure, view it through a different lens. Identify what went wrong. Was it marketing? Timing? Pricing? An honest assessment can uncover hidden insights, propelling you forward instead of dragging you down.

Take Risks and Learn - In the world of finance, taking calculated risks will yield great rewards. It's almost like a game of chess. You have to anticipate your opponent's moves while also positioning yourself for success. I've had my fair share of risky ventures. Some panned out beautifully, while others fell flat. But guess what? Every single experience brought me closer to financial wisdom. Don't shy away from such moments. Embrace them. They are opportunities waiting to unfold greatness.

When you hit a roadblock, remember, it's not about the fall. It's about the rise. Learn from both your successes and failures. Each lesson learned becomes a building block for your financial future. The beauty of this journey is that each hurdle can refine your vision and enhance your strategy. The path may be rocky but be rest assured that the view from the top is stunning.

6. Seek Mentorship and Guidance
We need each other. Surrounding ourselves with mentors and wise advisors can be a game-changer. Think about it: Why climb a mountain alone when you can have someone who's already been there showing you the ropes? Having a great mentor is like having a key that unlocks doors you didn't even know existed. Proverbs 27:17 tells us, "As iron sharpens iron, so one person sharpens another." This isn't just a cute saying; it's a powerful reminder of the influence and growth we can achieve when we connect with others who understand the path we're on.

Mentorship is crucial, but it's not just about asking someone to guide us blindly. It's about building relationships. When you find someone who resonates with your values—someone who shares your belief in the teachings of Christ—you cultivate a bond. You can bounce ideas off of them. Their insights can bring fresh perspectives. They can help you see your blind spots.

When searching for a mentor, don't just settle for anyone. Look for someone whose strengths complement your weaknesses. Maybe someone in your community inspires you. If you know a successful business owner in your neighborhood, consider striking up a conversation. Just ask them to meet for coffee or a quick chat. You might be amazed at how willing someone is to share their wisdom. Also, remember to pay it forward. While you're benefiting from the guidance of others, think about how you can lift someone else too. If you've learned valuable lessons, why not share them? It's fulfilling to be in a position to help others avoid the pitfalls you've encountered. Mentorship is a two-way street. It's about growing together in this wild world of entrepreneurship.

As Christians, we have a unique advantage. Our faith can guide us through the maze of financial decisions. Prayer opens doors that mere hustle often can't. When you're feeling lost, pray for guidance. Ask God to connect you with the right people at the right time. The universe has its way of connecting you with the right people, but you must be proactive in seeking that connection.

Trust in your journey. God places people in our lives for a reason. Whether they are mentors, peers, or even those who challenge us, each relationship can be a pivotal point on our path.

7. Stay Grounded in Faith

Above all, trust in God's plan for your life. Proverbs 16:3 encourages us to commit our plans to the Lord, and He will establish them. This verse is more than just words; it's a challenge and a call to action. When we anchor our plans in faith, we unlock doors that seem permanently closed. This doesn't mean we just sit back and wait for the heavens to drop our dreams into our laps. Instead, it's about taking those steps while letting God steer our unique path. As millennials, we often rush into hustling modes, piling debt on debt all while chasing the next shiny object. But living in God's purpose for our finances invites a deeper peace and assurance.

Consider your business plans or the side hustle you've been thinking about. How often do you pause to pray over them? How frequently do you reflect on whether these pursuits align with God's will for your life? When we include Him in our financial journey, we bring balance to our hustle. We cut through the noise and clutter that often occupies our minds when making decisions.

Sure, competition is fierce. The world of entrepreneurship can be harsh and unforgiving. But when we stay grounded in faith, we are reminded that what matters most is not the amount of wealth or success we accumulate but how we use it to make a positive impact in this world. So let us strive for financial success while keeping Christ at the center of it all. Let us trust His plan for our lives and commit our plans to the One who knows us better than we know ourselves. As we continue to grow and learn, may our faith remain the foundation of our financial journey, guiding us toward true abundance and fulfillment in His purpose for our lives.

3 Transferable Keys to Success

Focus, discipline, and consistency are not just buzzwords; they are vital tools in your financial toolkit. They are what will keep you steady on your journey as you learn to balance faith and finances. Lean into these keys and let God guide you through your entrepreneurial adventure.

1. Focus

Let's face it. The world is filled with distractions. Social media, the latest trends, and that nifty new gadget can all pull your attention away from what truly matters. But if you want to achieve anything—be it climbing that corporate ladder, launching your side hustle, or striving for a healthier lifestyle—you need to sharpen your focus. Take a moment to assess your current priorities. Are they directed toward your goals? Or are they scattered and chaotic, much like my attempts at a DIY project with a Pinterest board? Instead of mirroring someone else's success, keep your gaze fixed on what God has placed in your heart.

Create a plan tailored to your unique aspirations. If your aim is to grow your business, perhaps you can set dedicated hours each week for focused work. On days when temptation looms, remember Philippians 4:13: "I can do all things through Christ who strengthens me." This verse is your reminder that your power comes not from the pressure around you but from God within you.

2. Discipline

Discipline is the backbone of success. It means making sacrifices, which may include skipping the Netflix binge ("What a sacrifice!" you might exclaim) or decluttering your app folder. When I decided to launch my online course, I had to make hard choices. I cut back on late-night snacks and scrolling through social media platforms. Instead, I spent those moments writing content, crafting email templates, and praying for guidance.

Building new habits requires intention. Lay out your

intentions. Set a task list each morning to keep yourself accountable. Maybe you need to wake up a bit earlier or invest in a planner that can rein in your scatterbrained thoughts. In those moments of doubt and procrastination, remind yourself that Proverbs 12:1 tells us, "Whoever loves discipline loves knowledge." Knowledge doesn't just come from books; it comes from the everyday choices that build your future.

3. Consistency

There's a beautiful rhythm to consistency. It doesn't demand your perfection but rather your persistence. I always say, "You don't have to be great to start, but you have to start to be great." Whether you're applying this to your health, finances, or business, results come from repeated actions over time.

Picture this: You decide to create engaging content for your online course. On day one, you pour your heart into it. By day fifteen, you may feel tempted to skip a day or two. But remember that magic happens in the mundane. Each post and every interaction you have is a building block toward your success. I noticed those timely successes in my own life when I established a consistent writing schedule. The more I wrote, the more inspired I felt. Your momentum will build, and soon enough, you'll be riding a wave of achievement.

The entrepreneurial financial hardship journey can feel quite lonely. But remember, if God brought you to the mountain, trust that He will bring you through it. Each step will yield growth, and once you make it through, don't forget to thank God for the mountain!

Your financial path is not just about numbers; it's about purpose, passion, and living out His vision for your life.

EXPERT HIGHLIGHT
Tywone Thomas

Author I Entrepreneur I Business Coach
Buy Your Next Vehicle with Confindence Course
Website: www.cuautosearch.com/course
LinkedIN: Tywone Thomas Verified Account

Meet Tywone Thomas

Tywone Thomas is a seasoned entrepreneur and financial expert based in the Atlanta metro area. He is the Founder and CEO of Auto Assistance, LLC, a specialized auto-buying service that collaborates with credit unions to help their members navigate the car-buying process with confidence and ease. Through his work, Tywone has empowered countless individuals to make informed, financially sound decisions when purchasing a vehicle.

A passionate advocate for financial literacy, Tywone is the author of *10 Mistakes to Avoid When Buying Your Next Car*, a comprehensive guide that educates buyers on how to avoid common pitfalls in the car-buying journey. As the lead instructor of the auto-buying course *How to Buy a Vehicle Successfully*, he shares his wealth of knowledge and expertise with those looking to take control of their vehicle purchases while securing the best deals possible.

Tywone is deeply committed to helping consumers take charge of their financial futures, advocating for careful planning, transparency, and proactive decision-making. A family man, he lives in the Atlanta area with his wife of 20 years and their three children.

For more insights and resources from Tywone, visit www.cuautosearch.com/course.

Financial Wisdom for Car Buyers

When it comes to buying a car, one of the most important steps is to establish a clear plan before stepping foot in a dealership. Without a vision for your purchase, the dealership will create one for you. Starting with the end in mind and working backward ensures that you stay on track throughout the buying process.

If you plan to finance the vehicle, begin by determining the maximum monthly payment you're comfortable with, which should include not just the car payment but also insurance, gas, and maintenance costs. Once you have that number in mind, get pre-approved through a credit union—often the best option for financing.

When speaking with your loan officer, communicate your max budget clearly. For example, if you're aiming for a $400 monthly payment, ask what interest rate you qualify for and the longest loan term available. This will help you understand the total purchase price you can afford (including taxes and fees), as well as any restrictions on vehicle age or mileage.

By taking these proactive steps, you can approach the car-buying process with confidence, making informed decisions rather than being at the mercy of a dealership. This also benefits the dealer, as you'll arrive prepared and they can assist you in finding a vehicle that truly fits your needs.

Hidden Fees to Watch Out For

Rather than "hidden" fees, many buyers simply don't fully understand the charges listed on the bill of sale. Some fees are mandatory, while others may be negotiable. Dealerships structure their fees differently, so it's crucial to review them carefully before committing to a purchase.

One proactive step is to request a generic bill of sale from your sales representative before you visit the dealership. This gives you the opportunity to review the fees without feeling pressured on the spot. It also allows you time to assess and, if necessary, negotiate the fees before you even walk in, putting you in a stronger position as a buyer.

Leasing vs. Buying

Leasing versus buying is a common debate, and while leasing may work for some, I personally discourage it. In my view, leasing is essentially a glorified rental. At the end of the lease, you return the car with nothing to show for it. On the other hand, when you purchase a vehicle, you gain an asset that you can sell later, potentially recouping some of your money for your next purchase or savings.

While some people may find advantages to leasing, based on my experience, the downsides generally outweigh the benefits. It's important for every buyer to conduct their own research and determine what best fits their individual financial situation.

Thank You for the Mountain

ABOUT THE AUTHOR

In Thank You for the Mountain, Alicia Fitts conquers financial peaks with faith and fortitude.

In this riveting book, Alicia, a distinguished certified credit union financial counselor, invites readers on a transformative journey through the peaks and valleys of financial adversity. With unwavering faith as her compass and resilience as her guide, Alicia reveals life-altering experiences of how she scaled the daunting cliffs of debt to emerge victorious. She shows readers how they, too, can have their mountainous financial problems moved to succeed.

As the first African American and female assistant vice president of business development and community relations at a prominent credit union, Alicia's ascent to success was not without its challenges. Propelled by her steadfast commitment to her family—her devoted husband, Terrell, and their three cherished children, Noah, Evan, and Cassidy—Alicia fearlessly navigated the rugged terrain of financial uncertainty.

Recognized as one of Augusta Magazine's Top 10 in 10 Young Professionals to Watch and honored as Participant of the Year for the Columbia County Chamber of Commerce's Young Women on the Way program, Alicia's story is a testament to the power of determination and divine intervention.

Within the pages of Thank You for the Mountain, Alicia shares the invaluable lessons gleaned from her extraordinary journey. Through the lens of her profound relationship with God, she illuminates the path to financial freedom, offering sage advice and practical wisdom rooted in biblical principles.

REFERENCES

1. Osterland A. CNBC. 2019. *What the coming $68 trillion Great Wealth Transfer means for financial advisors.* Available from: https://www.cnbc.com/2019/10/21/what-the-68-trillion-great-wealth-transfer-means-for-advisors.html
2. Hanson M. Education Data Initiative. 2024. *Student Loan Debt Statistics.* Available from: https://educationdata.org/student-loan-debt-statistics
3. Rivera H, Wilbers P, Kantrowitz M. Bankrate.. *Student loan interest rates in November 2024.* Available from: https://www.bankrate.com/loans/student-loans/current-interest-rates/
4. Depietro A, Lapera G. Intuit Credit Karma. Credit Karma; 2022. *Average American Debt by Age and Generation: 2022.* Available from: https://www.creditkarma.com/insights/i/average-debt-by-age
5. Dickler J. CNBC. 2024. *Credit card debt hits a "staggering" $1.13 trillion. Here's why so many Americans are under pressure.* Available from: https://www.cnbc.com/2024/02/06/credit-card-balances-jump-to-new-1point13-trillion-record-at-end-of-2023.html#:~:text=Americans%20now%20owe%20a%20collective,the%20New%20York%20Fed%20found.
6. Channel J. LendingTree. 2024. *Mortgage Statistics: 2024.* Available from: https://www.lendingtree.com/home/mortgage/u-s-mortgage-market-statistics/
7. Horymski C. *Average Auto Loan Debt Grew 5.2% to $23,792 in 2023* [Internet]. Experian; 2024. Available from: https://www.experian.com/blogs/ask-experian/research/auto-loan-debt-study/#:~:text=The%20average%20auto%20loan%20balance,affect%20car%20buyers%20in%202024.
8. Hallie Davis AH. *Millennials' and Gen Z's Money Management During COVID-19: Challenges and Opportunities.* In: GFLEC

Working Paper Series. GFLEC; 2021. (2021-4).
9. Laurel Road. 2021. *Gen Z and Millennials Combat Financial Stress By Building Financial Habits to Achieve Mental Wealth.*
10. Ryu S, Fan L. The relationship between financial worries and psychological distress among U.S. adults. *Journal of Family and Economic Issues.* 2023;44(1):16–33.

www.ingramcontent.com/pod-product-compliance
Lightning Source LLC
Chambersburg PA
CBHW061736070526
44585CB00024B/2699